EVERY MAN
A KING

EVERY MAN
A KING

A Short, Colorful History of
American Populists

CHRIS STIREWALT

TWELVE

New York   Boston

Copyright © 2018 by Chris Stirewalt

Cover design by Adam Johnson. Cover photos by Getty Images.
Cover copyright © 2018 by Hachette Book Group, Inc.

Hachette Book Group supports the right to free expression and the value of copyright. The purpose of copyright is to encourage writers and artists to produce the creative works that enrich our culture.

The scanning, uploading, and distribution of this book without permission is a theft of the author's intellectual property. If you would like permission to use material from the book (other than for review purposes), please contact permissions@hbgusa.com. Thank you for your support of the author's rights.

Twelve
Hachette Book Group
1290 Avenue of the Americas, New York, NY 10104

twelvebooks.com

twitter.com/twelvebooks

First Edition: September 2018

Twelve is an imprint of Grand Central Publishing. The Twelve name and logo are trademarks of Hachette Book Group, Inc.

The publisher is not responsible for websites (or their content) that are not owned by the publisher.

The Hachette Speakers Bureau provides a wide range of authors for speaking events. To find out more, go to www.hachettespeakersbureau.com or call (866) 376-6591.

Library of Congress Cataloging-in-Publication Data has been applied for.

ISBNs: 978-1-5387-2976-2 (hardcover), 978-1-5387-2979-3 (ebook)

Printed in the United States of America

LSC-C

10 9 8 7 6 5 4 3 2 1

My dearest Newman and Arthur,

You have given your time and sacrificed my attention for this project. You have also—even without knowing it—helped me work out these ideas.

Keeping this republic will be your job, not mine. My generation is something of a historical pass-through in our country, bridging eras of momentous change. You are the ones who will get to decide what to do with this inheritance—the last, best hope of earth.

Knowing you, I could not be more pleased with our chances.

Gratefully,
Your loving father

Contents

EVERY MAN
A KING

"I've saved the lives of little children, I've sent men through college, I've lifted communities from the mud, I've cured insane people."

—Louisiana senator Huey Long in an interview with James Thurber for *The New Yorker*, August 1933

Introduction

There is something absolutely American about the notion that you, my friends, are getting screwed. Royally.

The fix was in even before you got here, so at least it's not your fault. In fact, you should count yourself lucky that you are one of the discerning few who understand how things really are.

And there's probably nothing you can do about it.

Unless...

The political idea that we now know as American populism is older than the republic itself, and certainly greeted that same republic with suspicion.

Merchants and planters and *elites* conspired against you even before they gathered in Philadelphia to draft the charter for these United States. Out in that same twilight space where legitimate concern still brushes past conspiracy theory, the proto-populists were already nodding knowingly.

As Bertrand Russell put it, "From the time of Jefferson onward, the doctrine that all men are equal applies only upwards, not downwards."

Or as one of populism's most vivid apostles, Huey Long, would more succinctly say, "Every man a king."

This energy has manifested itself in both parties and in various political ideologies over the centuries: conservatism, liberalism, nationalism, socialism, and even out-and-out bigotry.

But one constant has always been the fascinating assortment of charismatic leaders, characters, crooks, cranks, and sometimes charlatans who have—with widely varying degrees of success—led the charge of ordinary folks who have gotten wise to the ways of the swamp.

The depths of despair and heights of exhilaration with which Americans greeted the ascendance and presidency of Donald Trump were partly rooted in the idea that it was something altogether new. We've never seen anything like it before, they said.

But if you tug on one golden thread of Trump's presidential seal, you will find a cord running all the way back to the beginning of us.

Populist politicians have sometimes bedeviled us and sometimes saved us, but always fascinated us. And to understand our moment and what is likely to descend from it, we would do well to know some of those who have stormed the parapet before our current president made it over the top.

And as we come to understand these men, we also see that their successes and failures spring from some common traits and relied on some common circumstances in the republic and its people.

Every successful American politician has been some blend of democratic zeal and republican restraint. Our first partisan split—a clash between the factions of Thomas Jefferson and Alexander Hamilton—wasn't a struggle between opposing views as much as it was a conflict over emphasis (and always, always, always personalities).

Jefferson's idea of holding regular constitutional conventions might rightly be described as a perfectly republican idea. It's certainly a more populist concept than the permanent but amendable charter we ended up with, but Jefferson's automatic conventions would have most certainly made clear the primacy of the Constitution.

There's a reason why the party he founded once held both "Democratic" and "Republicans" in its name, you know.

Similarly, Hamilton owes his twenty-first-century vogue not to his sometimes breathtakingly elitist attitudes, like a nonhereditary kingship, but to his embrace of a culture of upward mobility and his vision of an activist, technocratic federal government.

(That and Lin-Manuel Miranda's ability to rhyme with "Rochambeau.")

Conservatives now mainly see the Constitution as a means to constrain the federal leviathan, while today's liberals tend to focus on the charter's guarantees of individual rights.

So it's understandable that modern Americans are prone to forget that the purpose of the document was to create a central government more powerful than all but a few of the revolutionary generation would have initially envisioned.

We believe now—as they did in the summer of 1787—that rightful government aims to produce the proper balance between freedom and order so that people are free to achieve their fullest potential. The tyranny of a despot and the tyranny of the mob are different in style but commensurate in their power to oppress and destroy.

In excess, both freedom and order can produce oppression. In equipoise, they produce miracles.

America's prosperity and progress toward equal freedom under the law probably owes more to our culture than to our government. We are not free because the government says so, but rather because we the people have been (mostly) able stewards of these historically unprecedented blessings. But even the strongest culture needs guardrails to provide predictability and keep us from veering too far from our objective of maximizing freedom and opportunity. When our culture and government are both healthy, their traits are complementary. But when either proves deficient, they can help prop each other up and help correct the maladies in one another.

James Madison was the Founding Father who would ultimately strike the balance between the young Jefferson's belief in the sovereignty of the commoners and Hamilton's desire for a federal government of real sovereign power. He was the one who best explained the way a government could be powerful enough to provide adequate security and protect individual liberty without becoming tyrannical itself: "Ambition must be made to counteract ambition."

By balancing powers between democratic institutions (such as the House) with republican ones (like the Supreme Court), the Founders created the governmental equivalent of a self-cleaning oven. There would be the rule of law to counteract popular excesses and popular sentiment to act against the abuses of the law.

The opponents of the Constitution, the Anti-Federalists, considered the argument a betrayal of the revolutionary spirit. At the debate in Richmond over ratifying the charter, Patrick Henry, the same man who had goaded his reluctant fellow Virginians into rebellion, led the charge against a strong central government. "Will the abandonment of your most sacred rights tend the security of your liberty?" he asked. "Liberty, the greatest of all earthly blessings—give us that precious jewel and you may take everything else."

Give him liberty or give him...

But in *Federalist* No. 45, Madison argues convincingly for a Constitution that would expand the reach of the federal government at the expense of the powers and autonomy of state governments. Madison explains that the rights, well-being, and happiness of the people supersede the more abstract rights the Anti-Federalists said they meant to protect.

"We have heard of the impious doctrine in the Old World, that the people were made for kings, not kings for the people," he wrote. "Is the same doctrine to be revived in the New, in another shape that the solid happiness of the people is to be sacrificed to the views of political institutions of a different form?"

Simply put, the purpose of the republic is not to maintain republicanism. Rather, a republican system is what history and our own experiences have shown to best temper the impulses of the electorate while still keeping the government accountable to the electorate's demands. The people can have what they want, but the process moves slowly because no branch of government can rule alone. If republicanism did not obtain the greatest portion of contentment for the greatest number of our people, we would long ago have scrapped it.

You have probably heard the old saw about thanking God for unanswered prayers. I certainly count as a blessing having not obtained many of the things that I, as a boy and young man, desperately wanted. And for other things, having to work and want for seeming eternities made me more grateful and better prepared to enjoy, steward, and exploit them.

Just as it's good that we as individuals don't get everything that we want, when we want it, it has proven to be overwhelmingly good that the American people's demands have sometimes been denied and are almost always delayed.

America didn't need petty fascism in the 1930s any more than I needed a brand-new car and the loan to go with it when I was fresh out of college.

That doesn't always wash with voters, though. In troubled and transformative times, especially, people have always and will always try to exceed what constitutional constraints will allow.

As the same fellow who wanted to make every man a king put it, "A perfect democracy can come pretty close to looking like a dictatorship, a democracy in which the people are so satisfied that they have no complaint."

Philosophers will always debate whether Plato was being ironic when he described the ideal system of government as essentially rule by a benevolent dictator. But Huey Long was most certainly not kidding when he imagined a perfectly contented people with—who else?—him as the supreme leader.

We venerate the idea that the people reign and broadly agree the rightful object of the government is the happiness of the people. But what do we do when what the people—or a number large and loud enough of them—want things that diminish the republican safeguards that keep us free?

And, conversely, what do we do when those republican safeguards help facilitate the abuses that cause the people to suffer? Consider this: The pro-slavery southerners who would found the same kind of decentralized confederacy rejected by the Founders in 1787 were masters of using delay and divided powers to protect slavery for decades prior to the Civil War. The ideological descendants of the people who opposed the Constitution because it favored the rule of law over the rule of the people were among the very best at using the law to maintain and expand slavery even when popular sentiment nationally had come to be harshly against the practice.

And at its best, American populism is about testing the idea that small-r republicanism is still in good working order. If we have a central government wholly beholden to the voting public and dedicated to preserving our natural liberties, it would be hard to get much momentum for a popular revolt. But when freedom and order are out of balance, watch out.

Some populist movements, like those of the Gilded Age and the Great Depression, have tended toward the more radical suggestion that the system itself ought to be scrapped. Those who today call themselves democratic socialists or economic nationalists are part of a long bloodline that stretches to the first colonies—those who say republicanism doesn't do the job.

Most populist outpourings, though, are aimed at either improving or restoring republican balance.

American populism emerges with the greatest vigor when those concepts are the most out of balance. Sometimes, the popular demand is for law and order imposed by a strong government. Sometimes, the demand is to tear down centralized authority. Sometimes, it's both at once.

This contradiction will be obvious to any Californian. In the Golden State, voters are given the most authority through direct democracy of any state in the union. You can get a referendum on the ballot more easily in America's largest state than in almost any other.

And what have voters done with their power? Proceeded to use it to repeatedly change even the most basic freedoms and institutions, often in antithetical directions.

Do you want more spending or lower taxes? Yes.

A democratic republic is not like Marshall Field's. The customers are not always right. You can't sustain high spending with low taxes or maintain reliable security with scanty government power. But offered as separate propositions, all of those things would be overwhelmingly popular, and not just in California.

That's why our system slows down the rate at which the demands of the people can be met. When I hear individuals complain about the speed with which Congress works, I am always tempted to remind them that the world has seen plenty of legislatures so efficient that they voted themselves right into oblivion.

It may take two years to get a post office renamed here, but it only took the Russian Duma a matter of months to make itself the vassal of Vladimir Putin. When it comes to government, speed kills liberty. A popular idea has to persist for long enough to defeat the barriers to change remaining in our system, and by then people tend to have either lost interest, modified the original aim, or are darned sure they really want it.

You might take a free sample of sauerkraut ice cream, but you probably wouldn't churn up a hand-cranked batch of it yourself on a whim. To do that, you'd have to be pretty sure that was exactly what you wanted.

The challenges placed before those who would enact the will of the people are intended to protect the rights of persons.

The primary objective of the Revolution was to end the oppression imposed by the British crown, but the urgent aim of the founding was to make sure that the aloof tyranny of George III was not replaced by the more intimate, more dangerous tyranny of the mob.

We would not need a Bill of Rights, or really any Constitution at all, if liberty were always preferable to the people.

It is common to hear about the rights Americans enjoy, but in truth, what we enjoy are the limitations on the power of the government, *even when* such exercise would be popular.

As we have witnessed over and over again, popular sentiment sometimes runs in favor of limiting certain kinds of speech or the practice of certain faiths, or otherwise abridging personal rights. Lots of things protected by the Constitution are unpopular. Which is exactly why we need it. You don't need rules to protect what's nice, easy, and popular.

That's why the Framers were so anxious about demagoguery. Their concern was that, like in Old World experiments with self-governance, politicians would succeed too well in inciting popular sentiment—using untruths and preying on emotionality instead of reason.

And hoo boy, they were right to worry. We've skated back from the brink a bunch of times in our history when the people demanded action beyond what our system and society allow.

That's why to tell you the story of what Americans are today, we're not going to focus on the men who crafted our system to balance republican restraint and democratic responsiveness. We're going to spend our time with those whose careers illuminate the power of individuals to harness popular sentiment to shift the balance between the two concepts.

The Framers were almost preternaturally prescient about how these opposing impulses and needs would play out. But ultimately, it was the people who have lived it—fighting savagely over how to best secure the blessings of liberty to themselves and their prosperity—who made American politics the house of horrors we all know and mostly all hate.

No, watching American politics melt down in the past decade like two scoops of sauerkraut sherbet on a July afternoon has not been fun.

But maybe it would feel a little bit better if you knew that not only have we melted down before, but that we drained all the way out of the cup and evaporated down to a sticky little spot on the sidewalk.

One of the things that most disturbs us about our moment is that, like every generation that has ever trod the sod, we are arrogant enough to believe we are always the culmination of history, rather than just one more stretch of a road that goes on forever.

Ozymandias had nothing on Americans when it comes to overstating the significance and permanency of our own accomplishments, even when the accomplishments are political dysfunction and civic misery.

Don't get me wrong: We're certainly not handling our new populist moment with aplomb, but neither has anyone else before us. And, blessedly, each similar spasm in our past has been a growing pain rather than a death throe—even when that was far less obvious in the moment than it is today.

Populism is both the symptom of and remedy to an imbalance between freedom and order in our society. The sentiments are always with us, but only certain circumstances allow for the rise of leaders who carry that message forward.

Sometimes they succeed in changing the system, but sometimes the system itself changes in the face of the threat of popular revolt. But all of the men and the campaigns we are going to be spending our time with in this book effected significant, enduring changes, including some that we have yet to see the full effects of.

We will run a currycomb lightly over seven American populist leaders. They run the gamut from unlikely vessels of popular sentiment to full-blown demagogues, lashing supporters into ecstasies of outrage and threatening to topple the very system itself. Some sought to restore order, while others sought to break it down.

But every one stemmed from that same belief that their supposed betters were trying to pull a fast one on ordinary Americans. And each one of them, quite oddly, can help us to better understand not just our current moment of populist upheaval, but what likely comes next.

First, though, you can't tell your populists from your plutocrats without a scorecard. So let's meet our team:

Andrew Jackson (seventh president of the United States)

b. 1767 (Waxhaws, Province of Carolina)

d. 1845 (Nashville, Tennessee)

There's embracing your outsider status and then there's horsewhipping a man on your town's main drag for insulting your wife. Donald Trump's putative favorite president, present company excluded, was a hard and exacting man. Jackson carried the scars of the American Revolution and fought entrenched interests in Washington with the same abiding hatred he carried for the British whom he defeated at the Battle of New Orleans. But his deep affection for those who, like him, were rejected by the eastern elite made Jackson the first and most successful tribune of the people. Jefferson imagined a day when the common people would choose a leader of their own, and Jackson was surely that. But unlike some who would follow him, Jackson nurtured his fire out of a desire to see the Founders' vision restored or preserved. Jackson was an innovator. He used new media—the lithograph was the Snapchat story of its day—and perhaps the first political team in the modern sense to sell his vision. By tapping into the unease and dissatisfaction of the members of the same wave of immigrants that carried his parents to the country, Jackson delivered a mostly peaceful revolution. We remember better today the savagery he visited upon other races than how he treated his own, but while Democrats may have taken his name off of the Jefferson-Jackson Day Dinner, they won't ever erase the way he made their party.

William Jennings Bryan (congressman from Nebraska)

b. 1860 (Salem, Illinois)
d. 1925 (Dayton, Tennessee)

Anybody can run for president three times, but what kind of party would nominate the same guy thrice? It's easy to say that today, but harder when you think of the stunning power of Bryan's oratory and his, dare I say, sex appeal. No, really! The Nebraska populist was a gripping, electrifying orator in an age when well-attended speeches and rallies made all the difference. "Crucify me on a cross of gold" was a hot number in 1896. Remember also that Democrats managed to elect only two presidents over the course of the seventy-one years between the start of the Civil War and the beginning of the Great Depression. The party couldn't find a way to fuse newly reenfranchised Confederates and northeastern immigrants. But Bryan, perhaps better remembered as the special prosecutor in the Scopes Monkey Trial after his political career was done, fused Christian moralism with economic liberalism to make a new, thunderous coalition. The Panic of 1893, the resulting depression, and a deepening chasm between the rich and poor had left a growing number of Americans doubtful of the promises of capitalism. Sound familiar? Before there was Bernie, there was Bryan.

Theodore Roosevelt (twenty-sixth president)

b. 1858 (New York, New York)
d. 1919 (Oyster Bay, New York)

Alexis de Tocqueville wrote that "a man's admiration for absolute government is proportionate to the contempt he feels for those around him." And boy howdy did the Rough Rider live up to that one. A child of great privilege from a wealthy New York family, TR looked like an unlikely populist. A guy who is said to have ridden horseback in morning clothes up the front steps at Fifth Avenue Presbyterian Church with his old Army buddies for his son's wedding doesn't exactly scream "man of the people." Roosevelt's unerring belief that he was right and almost everyone else was not just wrong, but probably stupid, propelled him headlong into the White House. For Roosevelt, populism was a means to an end: his modern, scientific, and progressive approach to government. How convinced was Roosevelt of his rightness? When his Republican successor backed away from TR's agenda, Roosevelt rode back in, tore the party asunder, and launched a third party in what may be the most damaging fit of pique in American history. And if you are ever tempted to believe that violence is a new addition to our political scene, remember that officials were so worried about violence from Roosevelt's fanatical delegates in 1912 that they hid barbed wire in the bunting at the GOP's convention in Chicago in case they rushed the platform when President William Taft was speaking.

Huey Long (governor, senator from Louisiana)

b. 1893 (Winnfield, Louisiana)
d. 1935 (Baton Rouge, Louisiana)

The senator from Louisiana famously got a black eye in the men's room at a swanky charity dinner out on Long Island in 1933. *Time* magazine, then a Republican house organ, had it that another guest refused to yield the facilities to the Kingfish and Long committed "a gross indignity" upon the trouser leg of the fellow, prompting the punch. This was the same dinner at which Long reportedly told a plump female guest as he snatched her plate,

"You're too fat already. I'll eat this." Of course, he cooked up a fantastic story about being jumped by a murderous gang in the washroom, fighting off his assailants, and being lucky to escape with his life. They were there to kill him because he was going to "share our wealth." Whether Long's adoring supporters, the ones he called "the boys at the forks of the creek," believed him or not, we don't know. What we do know is that they seemed to enjoy it, even if they knew they were getting taken. Long masterfully created a new permission structure for himself in which he could flout every rule; lie, cheat, and steal; and do it all in the name of sticking it to the man. The more the bluenoses in the newspapers howled, the better he liked it. And with his mastery of the radio, he could talk directly to his growing number of supporters across the country anyway. Why believe the lying press when you can hear it from the man himself?

George Wallace (governor of Alabama)

b. 1919 (Clio, Alabama)

d. 1998 (Montgomery, Alabama)

History rightly remembers the former Alabama governor as the last, most famous segregationist. He deserves that ignominy, but stopping there would let ourselves off too easily. Who Wallace was and what he discovered about American voters didn't end with the 1968 election. Legal segregation was already dead, but the deepening enmity between both major parties and blue-collar white voters was coming back to life. It wasn't just the desegregation of southern schools that got Wallace almost ten million votes across the country. It was anger. Wallace seethed alongside his voters who saw their country falling apart. Hippies. Women's libbers. One worlders. Pinkos. Black Panthers. And maybe worst of all, the elites who Wallace said were "looking down their noses" at decent, hardworking Americans. Wallace peddled easy fixes at home and abroad, all based on his slogan "Stand up for America." And his supporters knew exactly what he meant. In the end, union members melted back into the Democratic Party and suburbanites picked the safer course of Richard Nixon, who more subtly appealed to the same fears and resentments. But for a moment, in the summer of that dreadful year, anything seemed possible. Looking back, the most lasting political revolution of 1968 didn't take place in the streets of Chicago but was rather the one that Wallace led.

Pat Buchanan

b. 1938 (Washington, D.C.)

A woman, having talked warmly with Buchanan for some twenty minutes in one of the many television green rooms he has haunted for decades, asked a stranger the name of the man with whom she had been speaking. Thus informed, she paused briefly and said, "But he seemed so nice!" And he is. And he is also the grandfather of Trumpism. Just as much as Barry Goldwater's defeat in 1964 made way for Ronald Reagan, Buchanan's doomed charges against Vice President George H. W. Bush in 1988 and Bob Dole in 1996 were the genesis of Donald Trump's eventual primary victory. Buchanan coined the phrase "silent majority" to help his former boss, Richard Nixon, absorb the energy unleashed by George Wallace. And when his party's 2016 nominee discovered Buchanan's chestnut, Trump was choosing sides in the unresolved fight from two decades earlier. Reagan had brought peace between the feuding wings of the GOP: the libertarian-leaning economic conservatives and the nationalistic culture warriors. The Republican establishment was always more comfortable with the former, but Buchanan refused to go away quietly. He is as nice as that woman found him to be. But he is also the guy who proclaimed without irony about himself and his supporters that "we are building this Gideon's army and heading for Armageddon, to do battle for the Lord."

Ross Perot

b. 1930 (Texarkana, Texas)

It was altogether right that Donald Trump's first presidential run was as a candidate in Perot's Reform Party. The two billionaires are connected by much more than their many appearances on Larry King's TV show and their unusual hairstyles. One of the central tenets of American populism is that there is an easy answer, but that the people in charge won't use it out of greed, stupidity, or maybe just to keep you down. When he ran for president in 1992, Perot had answers. Lots and lots of answers—for the decline in manufacturing, for drug addiction, for health care, for congressional correspondence, for AIDS, for Japan's soon-to-be-dominant position in the world, for, well, everything. Like his forebear Teddy Roosevelt, and his heir Trump, Perot, a critic of an anachronistic Constitution, was convinced that the basic structure of the republic was unequal to the modern moment. The time had come for the "best people" to take the reins. In a series of thirty-minute infomercials, he laid out a vision for a new, pragmatic government that included a big dose of direct democracy in the form of "electronic town halls" in which television viewers would participate in presidentially directed plebiscites to decide major issues of the day. Press 1 to pass the budget. Press 2 to bomb Iraq. In the end, Perot's paranoia got the better of him, and, convinced that the CIA had infiltrated his campaign and was going to use doctored photos of his daughter to ruin her wedding, he dropped out of the race before dropping back in. What he didn't know was that he was just a little early to the party.

As they would say in Greenup: That's hotter than a two-dollar pistol, right there.

The lives of our seven subjects span more than 250 years, but they have operated on the same continuum and within the same system. They all succeeded in their revolts, but to widely different degrees and directions.

What they share in common, though, is their ability to convince millions of ordinary Americans of three things: that the system is rigged against them, that only these individuals can fix it, and that urgent action can still make every man a king.

CHAPTER ONE

Making Americans

(The Hard Way)

As Andrew Jackson was beginning his second term as president in 1833, the board at Harvard University thought it would be appropriate to bestow upon him an honorary doctorate of laws.

Law was the appropriate discipline, since Jackson had worked as a lawyer for decades in Tennessee, including a stint as a judge on the state supreme court. And the honorary nature of the award was just as appropriate, since Jackson had never set foot in a law school classroom as a student.

One tricky bit would be that Jackson would have to have a "discourse" with university president Josiah Quincy in Latin, but a few "res ipsas," a couple of "stare decisis" here and there, and a smattering of "mens rea" and it should all work out fine.

Quincy, though, wanted to tie the whole thing together by having his cousin John Quincy Adams on hand. Adams had beaten Jackson for the presidency nine years earlier after an Electoral College deadlock threw the contest to the House of Representatives, which chose the son of a president over the son of a penniless immigrant.

Jackson, never one to abandon a grudge, came back and not only beat Adams in 1828, he mopped the floor with him. Adams was summarily ejected from the White House by a mob of angry citizens, becoming only the second one-term president. The first, of course, being his own daddy.

When Adams's cousin came around to ask the former president to be on hand for the bestowal of the honorary degree, Jackson had just finished absolutely thrashing Adams's former secretary of state, Henry Clay, in the 1832 contest. Adams's party looked like dead meat and Jackson's political machine was intent on keeping it that way.

If Quincy had the gift of brain-dead jargon and buzzwords that now stultifies even the brightest minds in academia, he would have told his cousin that the event would provide "much-needed closure." It would also be a "win-win" since laureling Jackson would not only flatter the president but also demonstrate Harvard's status as the nation's premier educational institution—just tons and tons of synergies.

Adams, who served on the board but declined to vote on the question of the president's honorary degree, was not feeling it.

"I said that the personal relations in which President Jackson had chosen to place himself with me were such that I could hold no intercourse of a friendly character with him," Adams wrote in his very frank, very readable memoir. "I could therefore not accept an invitation to attend upon this occasion."

It wasn't just pique, Adams claimed. It was his objection to seeing the university debase itself and, to borrow another stultifying fake verb they'd use in Cambridge today, Jackson being "normalized."

This was before Harvard had given honorary doctorates to Placido Domingo, J. K. Rowling, and Oprah Winfrey.

Jackson would be joining a fraternity of letters that included not just Presidents Washington and Jefferson, but also Ben Franklin and, of course, Adams, his father, and their cousin Samuel. Jackson was most decidedly not their kind of people.

The former president recalled telling his cousin, "As myself an affectionate child of our Alma Mater, I would not be present to witness her disgrace in conferring her highest literary honors upon a barbarian who could not write a sentence of grammar and hardly could spell his own name."

Oh dear.

Adams was exaggerating. Jackson's correspondence shows him to be a clear, concise writer, though one who did struggle with spelling, having written of the continent of "Urope," an interest in "devilopment," and of the "femal" character.

Standards for uniformity in spelling were different in those days, and as a quick scan across social media will reinforce, bad spelling is with us always. There but for the grace of spellcheck go we all...

But not even Jackson's greatest admirers could have argued that the president, having grown up poor and ended any formal education when he was orphaned at age fourteen, was any kind of scholar.

But Adams's sneering was rooted in something else beyond the president's barbarism in politics and letters. Jackson was part of the vanguard of a wave of immigrants who were remaking the culture of the former colonies into something foreign and possibly quite dangerous in the minds of the coastal elite.

It's not surprising that as an unflinching, enthusiastic slave master and trader and as the engineer of the Trail of Tears, Jackson boasts few admirers in African American and Native American communities these days.

He may be the father of the Democratic Party as we know it, but his political heirs will sooner or later expurgate his legacy from mainstream American history.

Jackson may have been a wicked man—and by the standards of even fifty years later he would have been—but he is damned sure an immigrant success story.

Many populist politicians over the years have succeeded in exploiting native antipathies toward new immigrants. But only one president could say that he drew the strength of his populist revolt from the immigrants themselves.

For what's so breezily called "a nation of immigrants," Americans have had an awful time about the whole subject from the very start.

We are living now with the aftershocks of what is probably the fifth wave of immigration in U.S. history, and while the political turmoil seems dreadful, it's hardly the worst we've ever had it from either side of the subject.

Anyone who doubts it should read up on the Philadelphia riots of 1844 when nativists and immigrants fought with rifles and cannons in the streets of the heavily Irish Kensington neighborhood, where churches became armed camps and the streets were red with blood for weeks.

Philadelphia residents may feel tension between immigrant groups today, but all concerned, including the Dominican and Puerto Rican immigrants who live in Kensington today, wouldn't want to trade places with their forebears.

Sometimes these days, the mask slips and we hear the bad old words about the most recent wave of immigrants. Nativism is the cultural equivalent of an individual being startled. Our ugly snarl is rooted, as it always is, in fear.

Other times, we get the obverse: the angry resentments of the immigrant class and its progeny turning to radicalism or gangsterism. Before we had the National Council of La Raza and MS-13, we had Tammany Hall and the Molly Maguires.

We sometimes hear that America is a "melting pot," but it's probably better to think of us as stew rather than fondue. Yes, a new flavor informed by all of the ingredients emerges as we simmer, and the individual components are changed as they cook, but the carrots mostly stay carrots and the chuck roast mostly stays chuck roast.

It's in the gravy that results where we find the really good stuff. Just think of the music we have produced here that wouldn't be possible anywhere else: bluegrass, jazz, Tejano, show tunes, rock and roll, hip-hop, Gershwin, and on and on...

That's what we like so much about our culture. We have a great deal of regional cultural diversity in America. Go from Greenville, Massachusetts; to Greenville, South Carolina; to Greenville, Kentucky; to Greenville, Texas; to Greenville, California; and then try telling me that America is a homogeneous culture.

But even within regions and cities, we contain multitudes.

Is Boston an Irish city? English? African American? Italian? Caribbean? Portuguese? Indian? Yep, yep, yep, yep, yep, yep, and yep.

As it turns out, nearly four hundred years of attracting and assimilating immigrants will do that to you.

Our current populist revolt is substantially the result of our inability to assimilate the most recent wave of immigrants: Latinos, mostly of Mexican origin, who immigrated to the United States between the 1970s and about 2010. The wave crested in the decade of the 1990s with what the Pew Research Center estimates were 8.1 million new arrivals of Hispanic origin.

And this wave and the reaction to it have pretty well followed the playbook from the previous ones.

First, a combination of opportunity here and trouble abroad starts churning up some heavy demographic weather. The immigrants are initially welcomed as much-needed manpower for a growing economy. Then, as word gets around— be it in County Cork or Culiacán—the number of émigrés surges, creating real and imagined disruptions for the native population. This results in cultural and political backlash against that class of immigrants specifically and immigration generally. The circle is closed as the immigrants and their children establish their own political clout.

By the time the next wave is forming, some of the children and grandchildren of the previous one will be found shoulder to shoulder with other aggrieved native-born voters.

Your Italian American grandmother might not like seeing

so many Hispanic immigrants, but your Irish American great-grandmother may not have been too pleased about all the Italians and other Southern and Eastern European immigrants streaming through Ellis Island. And your German American great-great-grandmother might have been none too happy about all of the starving Irish pouring in during the famine years.

Nativism is a toxic by-product of something wonderful: the amazing speed with which immigrants and their families come to feel ownership of this nation.

By saying and believing the words of our American creed—"We hold these truths to be self-evident..."—first- and second-generation immigrants come to quickly feel entitled to these special blessings of liberty. To have a sense of ownership of our nation is the soul of self-government, that miraculous experiment in which we are continually engaged.

But that sense of entitlement sometimes means trying to pull the ladder up before the next wave can come aboard.

While elites tend to benefit from the availability of cheap labor, it's the folks farther down the ladder who are more likely to suffer economic and cultural consequences from wave migrations. So fears of scarcity, missed opportunities, and cultural shifts are among the most potent ingredients for a populist movement.

But not for Jackson. He was the wave.

Jackson's parents, Andrew and Elizabeth, and his two older brothers set sail for North America in 1765 from Carrickfergus, just above Belfast in what's now Northern Ireland.

Jackson's uncle had written of the opportunities in the Carolinas, as had relatives on his mother's side.

This was going to be a place where not only would they find the grip of the English crown to be lighter, but also abundant land and the freedom to practice their Presbyterian faith.

What they found was poverty, even more oppressive British occupation, and the same social stigmas attached to their dissenting form of Protestantism and culture as they had found back home.

The Jacksons were part of the Scots-Irish diaspora, estimated by the *Harvard Encyclopedia of American Ethnic Groups* at more than two hundred thousand souls, that poured like a river into the thirteen colonies starting in about 1680—perhaps the largest single unforced migration in history to that time.

At a time when the total population of our nascent nation was less than three million people, the Scots-Irish wave must've felt like a tsunami.

These were the descendants of mostly Scottish religious dissenters who had either been banished or fled to Northern Ireland starting in the 1500s. The English had devised a colonial plantation system to rule Ireland, and sending troublemaking Scots across the North Channel to subdue the Irish and work the land was an absolute two-fer.

But it was not a tranquil life. Here's how Jim Webb, a former Democratic senator from Virginia, described it in his history of the Scots-Irish, *Born Fighting*: "The wildest, most contentious people on all the earth, trapped in a sea-bound bottleneck, their emotions spattering out into poetry and music and brawls, calling each other Irish and Scottish now, or Catholic and Protestant, anything that might make another reason for a good, hard fight."

Those who fled the vicissitudes of such a life for North America, as Webb's, Jackson's, and my own ancestors did, found different scenery and greater opportunities but many of the same old problems they meant to leave in Ulster.

The elder Andrew died without property—possibly a squatter—on Twelve Mile Creek in the Waxhaw region on what's now the North Carolina–South Carolina border. His death came just weeks before his youngest son was born, thrusting a destitute Elizabeth and her infant son into the care of her sister and brother-in-law, for whom she essentially worked as a servant for most of her remaining days.

Elizabeth had high hopes for her youngest son, a boy of obvious keen intellect, and sent him for lessons at a nearby academy with the hope that one day he might become a Presbyterian pastor. It was not an ideal vocation for the head-strong boy.

"Even at a tender age," wrote Jackson biographer Robert Remini, "he swore a blue streak—fine, lovely bloodcurdling oaths that could frighten people half to death—hardly the language of a budding clergyman."

Jackson was eight years old when the Revolutionary War began. By the time it ended, he was a teenager, and his world and the world of his Scots-Irish countrymen was forever changed.

The influence of the Ulster Scots on the country as it was taking shape may sound outsized, but we should also remember that they paid for their chance in blood. And they were doing so for a new nation the leaders of which they held in almost the same level of distrust as they did the British.

Here's Webb on the subject: "The famed Pennsylvania line, perhaps the best unit in the regular Army, was mainly Scots-Irish. True to form, it is also remembered for angrily (and drunkenly) marching on the Continental Congress on New Year's Day, 1781, after not having been paid for more than a year."

The Jacksons certainly fit that mold.

Jackson's brother Hugh had volunteered for the Patriot cause and died of heat exhaustion following an ill-conceived militia attack near Charleston in 1779. And when the war came to the Waxhaws the next year, it came with bloody ferocity. British troops slaughtered dozens of surrendering Continental soldiers in what is now Lancaster, South Carolina. A young Andrew Jackson was one of the local Presbyterian congregants who tended to the wounded.

Sensing that she could not keep the war from them any longer, or perhaps them from it, Elizabeth Jackson sent both of her surviving sons to drill with the militia, where they were given duties as couriers, eventually seeing action in the Continental victory at the Battle of Hanging Rock in 1780.

The Jackson brothers were caught by British forces at their aunt's home the next year, which led to Jackson's legendary confrontation with an officer whose boots he refused to shine, earning the young man a slash from a saber and scars he carried on his left hand and forehead for the rest of his life.

Andrew and Robert were imprisoned in the notorious Camden Jail, where, subsisting on starvation rations, they both contracted smallpox. Elizabeth was eventually able to secure her sons' release, but it was too late for Robert, who died of the disease days after returning to the Waxhaws.

After Andrew had recovered, Elizabeth went down to Charleston to volunteer as a nurse tending to the cholera-stricken American troops aboard hospital ships in the harbor. She became infected herself and died in November 1781, just weeks after the decisive American victory at Yorktown.

The British had taken everything from Jackson, particularly a mother who came to represent a Madonna-like perfection to him. The vengeance he would exact for their perfidies would stretch out over decades and shape the course of American politics and world events.

But the war had given him a great deal, too, most of all the chance to rush through the Cumberland Gap into the waiting westward expanse of the new nation. He and his fellow Scots-Irishmen could finally be free of both British oppression and the social stigmas they faced from the eastern elite.

Census takers estimated that there were about thirty-five thousand people in the Western District of North Carolina, now Tennessee, in 1790. One of them was a twenty-three-year-old Andrew Jackson, now a young lawyer, who had secured a position as a frontier prosecutor.

By 1800, the new state's population had tripled from a

decade before and an increasingly prosperous Jackson was its first congressman.

But it was hardly just Tennessee. Racing out along the Ohio and Mississippi rivers and up their tributaries into Kentucky, Indiana, and Illinois, Jackson's Scots-Irish kinsmen, like one Thomas Lincoln, were spreading out into the vast interior.

And with the Louisiana Purchase in 1803, the flood rolled on into what would become Arkansas, Missouri, and what's now East Texas. Sam Houston and Davy Crockett joined Jackson in the pantheon of Scots-Irish frontier legends, and hundreds of thousands emulated their hard-charging approach to life.

Crockett, who would later part company with his patron Jackson over the treatment of Native Americans and other issues, took the following as his personal motto: "I leave this rule for others when I'm dead; Be always sure you're right— THEN GO AHEAD!"

(Yes, all caps was a thing before they invented Twitter.)

But it might also have been the motto for the entire new immigrant class of Ulster Scots. In spite of the disdain with which the rapidly expanding merchant and industrial centers of Philadelphia, New York, Boston, and Baltimore may have viewed them, this sense of urgent action in the face of uncertainty was forging a new American ethos.

As Webb put it, the Scots-Irish "did not merely come to America, they became America, particularly in the South and the Ohio Valley, where their culture overwhelmed the English and German ethnic groups and defined the mores of those regions."

Insofar as those mores included wrathfulness, cruelty, dueling, periodic indecencies, and a contempt for authority, it was not a perfect ethic for the new country. But Lord, it was useful for a nation in a hurry, as America always tends to be.

By the time of Jackson's first presidential run, the Scots-Irish may not have been the largest ethnic group in the country, but they had more than enough electoral clout to be heard. More important, though, they had changed the way every ethnic group viewed the shared national identity.

Jackson was only the first of more than a dozen presidents of Scots-Irish heritage stretching until the 1990s. But they did not win their victories by pure demographic arithmetic—not by a long shot. They won because of the success of Jackson and the members of his generation in defining American culture and politics.

Now, unless the United States finally decides to invade Canada to plunder its vast reserves of maple syrup and Bryan Adams albums, no other group of immigrants is going to get the same opportunities as the Scots-Irish did. They were first to the party and arrived without the same cultural and linguistic barriers that would impede the members of subsequent immigrant waves. That came with enormous benefits that went beyond even the cultural shift the Ulster Scots effected in America.

Consider the Germans, the next group to arrive en masse. It would be almost a century before the first German American president, Herbert Hoover, took office, and another generation after that before one with a still identifiably German surname, Dwight Eisenhower, came to power.

Irish Americans can claim only one president, and the descendants of the Ellis Island émigrés still haven't seen one of their own reach the pinnacle of power. Consider the fact that there has been an African American president in a nation frequently riven by racial unrest, but there still hasn't been an Italian American president after more than a century of immigration and assimilation by that community.

There's no question that immigrants to a well-established culture face different political challenges than those, like the Scots-Irish, who helped write the second draft of the book about what it meant to be American.

And yet the experience and success of Jackson and his cohort still proves instructive about the intersection of immigration and populism.

Whatever the relative disadvantages the members of the current immigrant wave and their children face compared to Jackson and his ilk, they share in common their demographic disruption and the power that it brings. It has been fashionable in the past several years to focus, usually with alarm, on the populist fervor driven by anti-immigrant sentiment. But that overlooks what's happening on the other side of the ledger.

The conventional wisdom holds that we are in a moment not unlike the turn of the previous century in which native-born anxieties about new immigrants, especially from China, fueled an ugly backlash in which leaders trafficked in bigoted stereotypes to drive their supporters into new ecstasies of outrage.

If populism is in its finest form when it reflects the desires of ordinary people to break through barriers imposed by a ruling caste, the lowest form of the philosophy comes when it is punching down onto those less fortunate and with even less influence in the halls of power. And the two impulses have often been inexorably intertwined in American politics.

The late nineteenth and early twentieth centuries are rightly remembered for the rise and ultimate triumph of organized labor in America. After decades of abuses by rapacious employers, trade unionists fought for and won protections that have long been enshrined in law, like the eight-hour workday, bans on child labor, workplace safety requirements, and a minimum wage.

But there was a strong dose of racist nativism in the tonic offered by labor populists.

Back in Nebraska in 1901 between his second and third presidential campaigns, William Jennings Bryan launched a newspaper aimed at his supporters across the country. He called it *The Commoner*, and it offered readers an easy-to-read format, a crusading zeal for pro-labor positions, and even some Sunday school–style Bible lessons from Bryan himself.

But it also offered plenty of fearmongering about Chinese immigrants.

The California gold rush and railroad construction had drawn large numbers of Chinese immigrants to the American West. By the 1880s it was thought that a quarter of California's workforce was Chinese, prompting growing demands in Sacramento for curbs on immigration from that country.

Local governments had long taken harsh measures against the Chinese, restricting where they could live or operate their businesses. But federal courts routinely struck down these regulations. It just wasn't possible to use ordinances to harass specific ethnic groups with the post–Civil War constitutional amendments in place.

But there was nothing unconstitutional about banning new immigration, and in 1882, Congress passed the first-ever legislation aimed at barring members of a particular ethnic group from entering the country. The Chinese Exclusion Act barred any immigration for a period of ten years. When the term expired, Congress not only reimposed the original ban, but added new requirements that Chinese Americans here legally carry citizenship papers at all times or face immediate deportation.

In 1901 the looming expiration of the Chinese ban became one of the hottest issues inside the American labor movement. Labor leaders warned that once capitalists were able to bring in cheap, highly productive Chinese laborers again it would mean disaster for white workers.

Bryan's Democratic platform of 1900 had called not only for continuing the ban on Chinese immigrants, but also for extending the restriction to "all Asiatic races." And in the fall of 1901, his newspaper took up the same cause with vigor.

In a front-page editorial entitled "The Yellow Peril," Bryan (or perhaps his brother Charles, who oftentimes wrote for *The Commoner*) inveighed for the imposition of a broader ban on Asian immigrants—Japanese and Filipinos being of particular concern—and against the idea that such people could be made American.

"A nation is under no obligation to the outside world to admit any body or anything that would injuriously effect [*sic*] the national family; in fact it is under obligation to itself not to do so," Bryan wrote to his devoted followers. "The influence of the United States will be much more potent for good if we remain a homogenous nation with all citizens in sympathy with all other citizens."

Bryan was making a moral argument for the exclusion on the grounds that a "distinct race like the Chinese" couldn't be in the United States "without exciting a friction and a race prejudice" among native-born Americans. That friction would weaken the nation, Bryan argued, would make America less able to do the good, moral, and Christian thing and help the Chinese in China rather than letting them besmirch our national family.

Bryan and his fellow Democratic populists got their way and the provision was made permanent in 1902, imposing restrictions that would remain in place until the 1940s when the United States was courting Chinese cooperation in the Second World War.

So is that the kind of outcome we are likely to see in relation to our current debate over Hispanic immigration?

We have already seen calls for an immigration "pause," as well as state- and local-level efforts to require suspected illegal immigrants to carry proof of their legal status at all times. We are often warned that this new era of populist xenophobia will result in the same kinds of abuses that Bryan and his cohorts visited upon Asians in America a century ago.

But from here, that doesn't seem like the obvious outcome. The experiences of Bryan and other populists from the turn of the last century would seem to be far less instructive than those of Jackson and his fellow Scots-Irish Americans.

The focus of the fight in the past decade has been over illegal immigration, and there has no doubt been a powerful populist response on the subject. But looking forward, it will be legal immigrants and their descendants who will shape the debate.

Almost one in five Americans now claims Hispanic origin, making them the second largest demographic group behind non-Hispanic whites. There will soon be sixty million Hispanic Americans, and the Pew Research Center found that half of all U.S. population growth between 2000 and 2016 was driven by Hispanics.

Also significant is that the main driver of that growth has ceased to be new immigrants but rather native-born Hispanics. As of 2015 more than two-thirds of all Hispanic residents of the United States were born here. And where that really matters is among younger Americans. The median age of non-Hispanic whites was forty-three in 2015, while the median age of Hispanic Americans was just twenty-eight.

The growth rate for the Hispanic American population has leveled off since 2010, but it's far too late for any Americans who harbor Bryan's sentiments about protecting the ethnic homogeneity of the "national family."

Census figures show that the Hispanic population in the United States grew by more than 1.1 million from 2016 to 2017 while the non-Hispanic white population actually shrank by about 10,000. The wave of immigration may have subsided, but the sea change in demography is only just beginning.

Americans have devoted much of our political energy of late looking to see who would be the new William Jennings Bryan of the white working class who would, like the progressive populists of a century ago, help suppress the disruptive competition of the most recent immigrant wave.

But America's first and most successful populist president understood where the peril lies for a republic like ours.

"It is from within," Jackson said in his farewell address in 1837, "among yourselves—from cupidity, from corruption, from disappointed ambition and inordinate thirst for power—that factions will be formed and liberty endangered."

Jackson had lived long enough to see his own tribe go from a disadvantaged ethnic subgroup reviled by both British colonial powers and the new American aristocracy to become the driving economic and cultural force in a rapidly changing nation. At the end of his own headlong charge into the elite, Jackson understood—and had the hard-won experiences to prove—that disharmony itself was the greatest threat to liberty. The better question for students of populism to be asking about the future isn't who will be the protector of disaffected white voters but rather who will be the Andrew Jackson of Hispanic America.

CHAPTER TWO

Money Matters

(Especially When It's Gone)

There is nothing like a good old-fashioned economic panic to get Americans ready for our preferred political gospel in hard times: share-the-wealth populism.

At the end of January 1894, with the economy in absolute ruins, populists in Washington were at the threshold of one of their long-sought goals: the imposition of an income tax on the wealthiest Americans. And the man with the ball was a thirty-three-year-old, second-term congressman from Nebraska, William Jennings Bryan.

Born in Illinois and only having moved to Omaha shortly before his first campaign, Bryan was an unlikely figure to be commanding the attention of the entire House of Representatives.

But lordamighty, the man could talk. And on the night of January 30, talk he did.

Remember, this was back in the day when speeches in Congress still mattered quite a bit. Before constant television coverage revealed our legislative branch to be populated by sleepy-looking older folks who appear to be watching a low-stakes gin rummy game rather than engaging in statecraft, Americans tended to care more about what members of Congress said.

And in turn, the presence of those cameras has tended to make the lawmakers themselves even more boring. Not only are they keener to avoid saying something that might—heaven forfend!—be novel, but they very much have an audience other than their fellow lawmakers in mind.

A congressman or senator today is thinking first about avoiding trouble by not committing a gaffe, but also of tailoring a message that will play to the folks back home in Grand Forks, Grand Rapids, or Grand Falls. Those kinds of messages do no good in convincing others in the body, since they are only thinking about the fine people of Sarasota, St. Paul, or Schenectady.

What passes closest to high-stakes oratory in Congress in our era are the interminable hearings on whichever topics the party in power happens to think will either harm the other side most or provide the necessary degree of posterior covering for their own patoots.

In our Washington, giant hot gusts of words are converted into pixels and beamed around the globe. This was supposed to provide the transparency and accountability that were absent when all we had was the *Congressional Record* and reporters' accounts to go on.

The mice in our marble Skinner box, though, quickly learned to say less and smarm more. In all but a vanishingly rare number of instances, what members say to each other is indistinguishable from the political palaver you hear in their media appearances, commercials, or campaign events. They are talking past each other to the voters and donors far from Capitol Hill.

"Debate" in Congress long ago came to mean the period of

time you have to wait before you vote exactly as you darned well knew you were going to anyway.

But not back when Bryan, "the Boy Orator of the Platte," took the floor.

(By the way, isn't it too bad that we don't give politicians nicknames like that anymore? "The Cicero of the Green Room" or "the Contribution Bundler of the Wasatch"? On second thought, maybe not...)

When Bryan spoke up that night, he didn't yet rate a full-blown epithet, but he'd be quite a bit closer when he was done. And given his flair for the dramatic, he was no doubt of a mind to make the most of it.

Americans were very much angry and afraid in those days, and with good cause. The economy had cratered after a financial panic the year before. Historians estimate that as many as one in five members of the workforce were unemployed.

The ones to blame were bankers, speculators, and a puny federal gold supply that had been badly depleted by the much milder panic of 1890. If you can't get poor Nebraska farmers mad at a plutocratic trio like that, turn in your populist card.

Here were the salt-of-the-earth yeoman farmers—the Jeffersonian ideal—ruined by bankers, swindlers, and sharps. Nebraska had been Republican from the start, but a righteous anger was tearing the state away from its abolitionist origins. Republicans had become the party of business, the new power in the rapidly industrializing nation. In the eyes of many out in the prairie and plains, that made Republicans the enemies of the farmer. And Democrats like Bryan were to receive them.

A little context may help here. Lowering the sky-high tariffs imposed by Republicans at the behest of eastern industrialists had been one of two animating causes for populists throughout the 1880s and 1890s.

Tariffs help manufacturers by jacking up prices on foreign competitors, but they hurt farmers by shutting off foreign markets when other countries retaliate. Farmers get hit with a double whammy because the same tariffs increase the prices of products and equipment they need.

When the government raises the price on foreign-made products and materials it means consumers pay more. Your neighbor might have bought a Massey tractor made in Canada while you bought a McCormick Harvester made in Chicago, but you both end up paying more because the price of the American-made product will float up almost to the price the government set for the import. That was great if you owned a tractor factory or maybe even if you worked in one, but not so much for the people who use them, as Bryan's constituents surely did.

But the even greater cause of the populists in Bryan's era was a demand for the government to devalue the dollar.

Inflation isn't popular unless you've got a debt problem, and after years of bad borrowing and bad weather, America's farmers were deeply in debt. The solution offered by populists was to devalue the currency by taking the country off the gold standard and increase the currency supply by backing American money with both gold and silver.

This would create a dollar that, as Bryan would say in his

1896 presidential campaign, "smiles upon the man who owes a debt as much as it does upon the man who holds a mortgage."

I'll let Kansas newspaperman William Allen White offer the conservative rebuttal to the populist demand for "bimetallism," with which Bryan would one day be synonymous:

> Legislate the thriftless man into ease, whack the stuffings out of the creditors and tell debtors who borrowed the money five years ago when money "per capita" was greater than it is now, that the contraction of currency gives him a right to repudiate. Whoop it up for the ragged trousers; put the lazy, greasy fizzle, who can't pay his debts, on an altar, and bow down and worship him.

There's harrumphing, and then there's Kansas Republican harrumphing! Though I will confess that "The Lazy, Greasy Fizzle" does sound like the name of a diner I'd like to try.

Even among Democrats, though, the idea of cheap money and rock-bottom tariffs was hardly universal as Bryan was stepping into the arena. And those divisions were about to get sharper once President Grover Cleveland was back in power.

Cleveland was a Democrat, but he was also a classical liberal of the Jeffersonian mold who was highly skeptical of activist government at home and abroad. There's a reason he still holds the single-term record for presidential vetoes at a cool 414.

He and his ilk were sneered at as "Bourbon Democrats," a

dig at the Versailles-like detachment their populist rivals saw in them.

While Cleveland and his fellow Bourbon men (Washington is always populated with plenty of those, whoever's in power) favored lower tariffs over the managed economy preferred by the Republicans of the day, he didn't want to go as low as Bryan and the other insurgents. And he was not interested in further devaluing the currency.

The populist movement of the era was born out of the shared frustrations of the agrarian West, which in those days more or less started at the Mississippi, and the still-suffering South. Farmers' debts and tariffs that were blamed for weak agricultural exports and high consumer prices were understandably at its center. These ideas were the rocket fuel that relaunched the Democratic Party after decades lost to rebellion and reconstruction.

Cleveland, a New Yorker, had a different view than the Prairie Populists who actually provided the electoral energy that made him the only Democrat to become president over a span of fifty-two years.

And when he lost after his first term, it looked like that unhappy coalition of still-resentful southerners, new immigrants in the Northeast, and poor farmers in the Midwest was kaput.

The financial panic of 1890 had started to change those considerations, though. Republicans got routed in that year's midterm elections as the party, its leader President Benjamin Harrison, high tariffs, and dear money all took it on the chin.

The wave swept ninety-three House Republicans out of office and brought in new Democrats, many, like Bryan, from across the plains. Eight members of the new Populist Party even washed up on the banks of the Potomac.

Despite Cleveland's singular accomplishment in 1892 of winning two nonconsecutive terms as president over the beleaguered Harrison, Republicans regained some ground in Congress. This was thanks in part to the addition of twenty-four new House seats after the 1890 census to better represent the country's booming population. Those seats happened mostly to be in more prosperous, more Republican parts of the country.

After the election, the Democrats were back in charge at both ends of Pennsylvania Avenue, but all were acutely aware that their perches were precarious.

That awareness grew into outright alarm ten days before Cleveland took office for the second time when the Philadelphia and Reading Railroad went bust. It was a beginning of a financial panic and economic collapse that would rival the Great Depression for intensity, if not duration.

Railroads had overbuilt during the boom years after the Civil War, and when those same struggling farmers couldn't pay their freight bills anymore, railroads started bankrupting in bulk.

The Northern Pacific; the Union Pacific; and the Atchison, Topeka and Santa Fe railroads all went down, dragging down the banks that backed them, too. Even before Cleveland and his party could really get under way, the economy was burning to the ground and without a fire crew to douse it. There was no Federal Reserve to provide emergency liquidity, no federal regulations that required banks to capitalize at certain levels, and no FDIC to bail out depositors.

And what better to do when your party has its back up against the wall than to engage in savage internecine warfare?

The panic proved useful for Cleveland initially, since it helped him convince loose-money Democrats in Congress to actually *tighten* monetary supplies. A law passed three years earlier as a sop to the populists had made it possible to redeem silver for paper money. When the have-nots showed up with silver, banks were obliged to pay out, even unto the point of death.

By repealing the Sherman Silver Purchase Act, Congress did help stop the financial meltdown, sparing the middle-class families who feared for their life savings and keeping credit flowing to some degree. But as panic turned into depression, populist Democrats were losing their patience with their president—especially since they believed his dear-money policy was holding wages down.

Cleveland had kept the economy afloat, but the boat was leaking badly.

It's important to remember here just how bad that depression was. Under very similar circumstances in 2009—a steep recession that followed a financial panic triggered by the busted bets of speculators and banks—unemployment reached 10 percent for exactly one month in October of that year.

Economic historians disagree on their estimates about the

catastrophe that followed the Panic of 1893—was the peak 19 percent or 17 percent or something else?—because we didn't keep track of unemployment the way we do now (until people started collecting unemployment insurance).

But there were certainly more than five years of double-digit unemployment.

In 1894, the country was convulsed by strikes, riots, and demonstrations. The *New York Times* reported that some two hundred thousand miners in eleven states went out on strike to protest their wages. Violence broke out between strikers and authorities in Uniontown, Pennsylvania, LaSalle, Illinois, and Belmont County, Ohio.

In fact, as Bryan was giving the floor speech that would change his career and, by extension, American populism on that January night, one of the ugliest labor disputes of the era was taking shape at gold mines in Cripple Creek, Colorado, complete with dynamite attacks, shootouts, and an attempted lynching of the state's populist governor.

Even so, Cleveland and the moderate Democrats weren't going back to bimetallism with the economy still failing so badly. That left the tariff question as the main flashpoint in the party. That fight would drag through most of the year before reaching an unhappy ending for all involved.

But there was something else. Something more viscerally connected to the anger and, most of all, resentments of poor folks. And unlike the cheap money gospel preached by the farm, it would get amens from poor folks in Omaha, Atlanta, Boston, and Tammany Hall: Spread the wealth around.

Whether you were the son of Irish immigrants working as a day laborer on the docks in Boston, the son of Confederates chopping cotton in the Arkansas Delta, the son of West Virginia mountaineers shoveling coal in a coke battery in Pittsburgh, or the son of Scandinavian sodbusting homesteaders trying to get winter wheat to sprout in Minnesota, you could all agree on one thing: The Gilded Age wasn't so glittery from your end of things.

In 1896, according to the gripping PBS documentary *The Gilded Age*, about four thousand American families controlled as much wealth as the other 11.6 million put together. We talk a great deal these days about "the 1 percent." Well, how about the .034 percent?

The panic didn't put a hitch in Cornelius Vanderbilt II finishing in 1893 what historians still say is the largest private home ever built in New York City, a 130-room monstrosity at the intersection of Fifth Avenue and 57th Street built to look like the Château de Blois in the Loire Valley of France. It was on a lot now occupied by the more modest edifice of Bergdorf Goodman's.

But if you were a factory worker who saw what the National Bureau of Economic Research said was a 5 percent drop in real wages from 1893 to 1894 when your family was already getting by on perhaps a dollar a day, you surely noticed when boom went bust.

Princeton University historian Nell Irvin Painter described the Gilded Age this way: " 'Gilded' is not golden. 'Gilded' has the sense of a patina covering something else. It's the shiny exterior and the rot underneath." And those folks subsisting in the rot knew it.

Not only would an income tax satisfy those ready to take up pitchforks, but it would also help defeat the argument against lower duties and tariffs which held that the federal government couldn't afford to forfeit the revenue. That's why populist leaders inside and outside the Democratic Party had spent more than twenty years fighting for a tax on the rich after Congress repealed the special tax on income it had levied to finance the Civil War.

With no explicit constitutional provision for such a tax and considerable opposition from not just the booming business class but also the heirs of Jacksonian populism who were worried about giving the federal government too much power, the idea had languished.

But the populist fire was burning stronger than ever, and the income tax was one of the hottest coals in the furnace. And don't you think for a second that Bryan didn't know that well when he started his crusade.

Aimed at what lawmakers estimated was a group of just about eighty-five thousand of the richest households in the country, the tax would levy a rate of 2 percent on income beyond $4,000 (more than $100,000 in 2018 dollars).

A tax of 2 percent only on earnings beyond your first $100,000 sounds like almost no tax at all today. But the other side of the debate in 1894 saw it as creeping communism.

Representative Bourke Cockran, a Democrat from New York, and most definitely of the Bourbon variety, rose on the night of January 30, 1894, in opposition to Bryan and the taxation brigade. These men, he said, were violating a core American value of equality in the eyes of the law.

Cockran, thought to be the best orator in the House at the time, denounced the plan as "not imposed to raise revenue, but to gratify vengeance. It is not designed for the welfare of the people of the whole, but for the oppression of a part of the people."

Bryan had his own ideas about the oppressed part of the people, and he thundered. We don't know what he sounded like that night, of course, but we know how his oratory was generally received.

"By George," his fellow populist Teddy Roosevelt would later mockingly say of him, "he would make the greatest Baptist preacher on earth."

Bryan was, like Roosevelt, a Presbyterian. But while Roosevelt was of the modest, decorous kind, Bryan was full of the same zeal as their coreligionist Jonathan Edwards. To him, Americans were still "sinners in the hands of an angry God," but the nature of the sins were economic in nature.

This is, after all, the man who accepted his first presidential nomination saying, "We will answer their demand for a gold standard by saying to them: You shall not press down upon the brow of labor this crown of thorns, you shall not crucify mankind upon a cross of gold."

But on that January night, and still a relative unknown, Bryan was feeling more of an Old Testament vibe as he rose to answer the great Cockran.

"Mr. Chairman," he began, "if this were a mere contest in oratory, no one would be presumptuous enough to dispute the prize with the distinguished gentleman from New York; but clad in the armor of a righteous cause I dare oppose myself to the shafts of his genius, believing that pebbles of truth will be more effective than the javelin of error, even when hurled by the giant of the Philistines."

Well, now...

Bryan would go on (and on and on) in a speech where he, the little David from Nebraska, would hurl many pebbles at the Goliath of New York. In fact, he used everything within reach. There was humor, flattery, indignation, and even a verse from Walter Scott's famous poem about patriotism:

> *Breathes there the man, with soul so dead,*
> *Who never to himself hath said,*
> *This is my own, my native land!*
> *Whose heart hath ne'er within him burn'd.*

With a penchant for the statistical (whether accurate or not) that populists of every era seem to share, Bryan tacked up the hides of those who would protect the plutocrats from paying their fair share.

"Ninety-one percent of the 12,690,152 families of the country own no more than about 29 percent of the wealth," Bryan said the night of his rapture. "And 9 percent of the families own about 71 percent of the wealth."

Can't you just hear him spitting out those digits like nails?

Imagine the precise, clipped midwestern diction taught to him by his politician father, an Illinois state senator and circuit judge, and his mother, who Bryan said made him recite his lessons as a little boy while standing atop the kitchen table.

"Twelve million, six hundred and ninety thousand, one hundred and fifty-two..."

Auburn University economist David Whitten wrote about how the era of financial panics shaped American politics. I think you'll recognize our man in the midst:

> Those whom depression struck hardest, as well as much of the general public and major Protestant churches, shored up their civic consciousness about currency and banking reform, regulation of business in the public interest, and labor relations. Although nineteenth century liberalism and the tradition of administrative nihilism that it favored remained viable, public opinion began to slowly swing toward governmental activism and interventionism associated with modern, industrial societies, erecting in the process the intellectual foundation for the reform impulse that was to be called Progressivism in twentieth century America.

Bryan was hammering out a new gospel that night in the House of Representatives, and though it may have long been denuded of its Calvinistic origins, it's the same one you could hear today from Bernie Sanders.

Bryan's speech—and, doubtless, a desire by some of Cleveland's allies to placate the populists there rather than on the gold standard and tariffs—carried the day, and Congress would go on to approve the first peacetime income tax, which the president dutifully signed.

Yes, Cleveland signed rather than vetoed a bill for a change. But he did so with the expectation of what would happen next: swift legal challenges and a just-as-swift overturning by the Supreme Court the next year. It would take the populists nineteen years and a constitutional amendment to finally obtain what Bryan thought he won that night.

But as far as the gentleman from Nebraska was concerned, there was no court in the land that would be able to stop the phenomenon that so intensified the night of January 30, 1894. In less than three years, Bryan would be his party's nominee for president (the first of a record-setting three failed general election losses) and his once-radical preachments became Democratic doctrine.

Without the successive panics and recessions that first got Bryan to Washington and then gave him his magic moment that night in the House, the world may never have met "the Boy Orator of the Platte." And without the financial calamities that rocked the nation's economy again in 1896, and with almost equal destructiveness as the 1893 panic, in 1907 he could have never so thoroughly conquered his party.

In that, Bryan keeps company with Huey Long, who really *did* talk like a Baptist preacher when he went to war against

Teddy Roosevelt's cousin Franklin in 1936 ahead of the second, and arguably more painful, dip of the Great Depression.

Long, like Bryan, made the most of his brief time in Congress. But while Bryan shied away from accusations of socialism and radicalism, the former Louisiana governor embraced them when he got to Washington, even unto defending the idea of a popular dictatorship and calling for collectivism and the confiscation of wealth.

Given their rhetorical skills, Long and Bryan might have been successful politicians without panics, crashes, and depressions. And we can't know if they could have used some of the other populist rocket fuel to ride to national acclaim. But we know at least that the combination of men and moment produced two of the most radical economic platforms ever to make it into the mainstream.

But every major eruption of populist sentiment in American history has included a strong dose of economic resentment. In the second half of the twentieth century and today, the sense of economic grievance has been intense, even when the national economy has been healthy.

Consider the national debt, a matter of great concern when Ross Perot launched his first presidential bid in 1992, but essentially disregarded today. Now both parties embrace the miraculous works of cheap debt and have ready explanations for why the federal government having obligations more than five times its annual expenditures is really the smart thing to do.

Governments carrying too much debt are like bookkeepers

who embezzle. It works great right up until it doesn't. And when it doesn't, boy, look out.

When Perot was running, though, the country wasn't suffering many consequences from a debt that was a fraction of what it is today. But to Perot, the debt was evidence of what he said was chronic mismanagement, and, when paired with dire warnings about the danger of free trade, a warning sign of an impending crash.

One of the good things about running as a populist firebrand is that if the present doesn't offer you enough disasters to exploit, you can always invite your supporters to live in the imaginary disasters of the future.

Other times, economic issues can be amplifiers for more potent cultural issues.

Pat Buchanan wanted to help the "hard hats" with protectionist proposals in his own presidential run. But when he as a speechwriter was helping President Richard Nixon navigate the intensifying culture war around the Vietnam War in 1970, and a group of New York construction workers roughed up some protesters who were burning the American flag, it was about the hard hats, too.

In his memoir, *Nixon's White House Wars*, Buchanan recalls hearing an argument that the administration should come down on the side of the protesters.

"The most insane suggestion I have heard about here," he wrote, "was to the effect that we should somehow go prosecute the hard hats to win favor with the kiddies."

Buchanan had what he said was a better idea: Weaponize

Vice President Spiro Agnew to attack the same dominant culture that looked down on those construction workers. Executed correctly, he argued, the vice president's message "would have hit every blue-collar worker in the country and these are our people now—if we want them—and frankly they are better patriots and more pro-Nixon than the little knot of Riponers we have sought to cultivate since we came into office."

If you want the support of blue-collar workers in the culture wars, a good place to start is with economic policies aimed at blue-collar workers. Or, conversely, once your political movement comes to depend on the votes of the white working class, your economic priorities will come to reflect theirs.

There are many reasons why Bryan never reached the pinnacle of power. His religiosity and zealous moralizing probably played considerable parts. So too did the narrowness of his focus. Bryan took a turn as secretary of state after his third presidential defeat, but he would always be to voters the friend of the farmer, the one who would not be crucified on that cross of gold.

But he was also a victim of the political realities of the era. Bryan may have had misgivings about the effects on American culture and values from the increasingly large numbers of immigrant arrivals, but his party surely needed their votes.

Franklin Roosevelt was a finer politician and better rounded in his skills than Bryan. Roosevelt was also a far less radical thinker. But in the seventy-two years between the first elections of Lincoln and FDR there were plenty of other fine, well-rounded mainstream Democratic politicians who sought the presidency. Yet only two Democrats won the White House, and in the case of Woodrow Wilson in 1912, it was a fluke made possible by a Republican schism.

So no, populist success doesn't depend entirely on financial panics or depressions, but on the left and the right there are few energies as powerful as the sense of economic grievance. And when that grievance is tied to real or perceived abuses by elites, it is a force multiplier for any populist movement.

And if that is coupled with the kind of desperation that hard times can produce, you have the alchemy that makes previously impossible ideas sound mainstream.

CHAPTER THREE

Social Climbers

(Transitory States)

The Republican Party as we would know it for a century was born in a "human cauldron that was boiling all around" at the Chicago Coliseum on the week of June 16, 1912.

Hundreds of uniformed police officers prowled the aisles looking for weapons brought from outside or improvised on the premises—even a placard holder can make a pretty good club in the hands of a dedicated user—and groups of delegates massing to charge the platform.

And if the visible deterrents weren't enough to keep the crowd from becoming a mob, there were plainclothesmen milling in the crowd, well-armed men behind the stage, and barbed wire hidden in the bunting in front of the rostrum. If this floor fight turned into the real thing, convention organizers and police were ready to use deadly force if necessary to keep order.

In an era of political assassinations at home and revolutionaries abroad, the possibility that the GOP convention could devolve into violence wasn't an idle fear.

"It is almost incredible to hear at a national convention the question seriously discussed if there will be firearms used and whether blood will be shed," reported the *Washington Post* at the time. "But one can hear this at every step in the frightful jam and welter in the hotel lobbies."

The man who set the cauldron to bubbling had about as unlikely a résumé for a revolutionary as you can imagine: a former two-term president, former governor of the largest state in the nation, and a member of one of the nation's wealthiest, most influential families.

But those kinds of expectations were meant for lesser men than Theodore Roosevelt. The standards of restraint and decorum that governed others of his class simply did not apply to someone who felt the weight of destiny as Roosevelt did. He was "the man in the arena" and didn't give a whit about norms and critics, since he was the one willing to stick his neck out.

This was the guy who on his ill-conceived but astonishingly lucky charge up San Juan Hill during the Spanish-American War—the charge that would make him a national hero and launch his political career—turned, out of breath but grinning widely, to his aide and said, "Holy Godfrey, what fun!"

In Chicago fourteen years later, Roosevelt had lost none of his boldness (nor his recklessness) from San Juan. While he may have tried to be a bit more restrained during his time in the White House, the Rough Rider had returned from a brief, unhappy retirement ready to do battle against his party, his friends, his successor—anyone who would resist his charge for a new, progressive populism. He would not make the mistake of moderation again.

"Fearless of the future; unheeding of our individual fates," Roosevelt, well aware of the possibility of violence, told the throng outside his hotel near the convention hall. "With unflinching hearts and undimmed eyes; we stand at Armageddon, and we battle for the Lord!"

No wonder they put the barbed wire in the bunting...

So how did Roosevelt go from esteemed former president, Nobel Peace Prize winner, and father of America's national park system to a guy standing on a balcony of a Chicago hotel roaring at a group that certainly included some would-be hooligans about the Battle of Armageddon?

To understand him in context, let's first go back before his presidency, before his rise in New York politics, and before his military adventures in Cuba. Let's go back to the world that made him.

Young Roosevelt doesn't look like he would have made much of a populist. Born into astonishing wealth in Manhattan at a time when New York was stretching itself into the American colossus it would become, "Teedie" should have followed in his father's footsteps.

Like Theodore Roosevelt Sr., known to his family as "Thee," the younger Roosevelt should have been preparing to manage the family business of importing plate glass, tending to its expanding fortune, and devoting himself to those worthy causes favored by his father, like the Children's Aid Society and the Metropolitan Museum of Art.

Now, I do not hold that American populism is exclusively the domain of southerners. But I will insist that the American South provides a particularly nurturing environment for populist sentiment. From the Anti-Federalists who opposed the Constitution, to the Jacksonian upstarts who made the

Democratic Party, to the ravening fires of secession itself, to Huey Long's bayou empire, to George Wallace's assault on northern elites, and even to every modern Republican primary election, populism grows like kudzu down south.

And what you may not know is that Teedie's mama was a Georgia girl through and through.

Roosevelt's many and mostly adoring biographers tend to focus on the degree to which his family's Dutch asceticism and the physical rigors of muscular Christianity at home and at Harvard transformed an asthmatic weakling into the brawny hero of San Juan Hill. That's all fine, but it does tend to give short shrift to the importance of his adored and revered mother, Martha "Mittie" Bullock Roosevelt.

David McCullough's excellent biography of a young Roosevelt, *Mornings on Horseback*, does not miss the mark:

> Guns, violence, savage death, episodes that seemed more like the stuff of fable or fantasy, were all part of the world Mittie spun.... She could portray in marvelous detail how a pack of bloodhounds pulled a cougar to pieces or describe the midnight death struggle between a cougar and a half-naked black man, one of great-grandfather Daniel Stewart's slaves, a story the impressionable little Teedie would remember all his life.

I can't say for certain that Roosevelt Jr. wouldn't have ended up the hell-raiser he became if his father would have done as his peers did and taken a more modest Dutch bride, but I tend to believe that Roosevelt Sr.'s choice to import a romantic, lyric daughter of the South made the difference for Teedie and American history.

Of course, romanticism and bloodlust alone won't carry you as far as they will if you pair them with extraordinary wealth and intimate access to power.

TR's hard-charging approach to politics and life was a luxury afforded to him by generations of Roosevelts whose wealth and influence would shield their scion and give him room to maneuver through a changing political world. So sure of himself was Roosevelt, now "Teddy" to his friends, that he dropped out of Columbia Law School after just a year so that he could seek and win a seat in the state assembly.

Privilege also shielded Roosevelt when tragedy struck on February 12, 1884. His beloved mother and his wife of just four years died on the same day. Mittie succumbed to typhoid fever early that morning, and his wife, Alice Lee Roosevelt, who had just given birth to the couple's first child two days earlier, passed away in the evening.

That is not to say that Roosevelt did not suffer terribly for his dual losses. But how many twenty-five-year-olds could've taken off the better part of two years to work through their grief on a ranch they already owned in the Badlands of the Dakotas?

When he returned from his time of hunting, cow punching, and even a stint as a frontier sheriff, Roosevelt channeled his prodigious energies into two new projects. First, another marriage, this time to childhood sweetheart Edith Kermit

Carow. She would bear him five more children, whom they would raise alongside the daughter from his first marriage.

Second was a frontal assault on New York politics.

In eleven years, Roosevelt went from a failed bid for New York mayor to assistant secretary of the Navy. That was the job he left to help form the Rough Rider regiment of aristocrats, cowboys, and other ne'er-do-wells who won glory on San Juan Hill during the Spanish-American War. His battlefield fame combined with the able ministrations of New York's increasingly powerful Republican machine made Roosevelt governor at just forty.

Machine Republicans, however, found Roosevelt a more appealing candidate than officeholder, as he would oppose many of their most cherished initiatives. One of Roosevelt's twentieth-century successors in Albany, Mario Cuomo, famously said, "You campaign in poetry. You govern in prose." Roosevelt could better be said to have done both things in the style of a zealous auctioneer: fast, loud, and sometimes hard to follow.

Rather than face the prospect of another term with their rambunctious young governor, party bosses conspired to kick Roosevelt upstairs to the vice presidency in 1900. National Republican kingpin Mark Hanna of Ohio had other ideas, but found himself outmaneuvered by the eastern Republicans, led by Senator Henry Cabot Lodge of Massachusetts, at the convention in Philadelphia that year.

Roosevelt may not have been his first choice, but Hanna needed a new running mate for President William McKinley's reelection bid. Vice President Garret Hobart had died the year before and Roosevelt, like New Jerseyan Hobart, would balance out the ticket geographically with Ohioan McKinley, but also add youthful verve to the impossibly dignified incumbent.

Hanna may have thought Roosevelt a loose cannon, but it did not much trouble the boss. In those days, as it is now, vice presidents can easily be made into potted plants—warming seats at state funerals, "reinventing government," sucking up to local politicos, or some other busywork.

History had other plans.

On September 6, 1901, Leon Czolgosz stood in a line of well-wishers at the Pan-American Exposition in Buffalo, New York, for the rare chance to see McKinley in person. Czolgosz waited his turn and then stepped forward clutching a .32 caliber Iver Johnson pistol and fired two shots at point-blank range into the president's midsection. McKinley would die eight days later from his septic wound.

A man of less self-regard than Roosevelt might have been humbled by being so quickly and violently thrust to the pinnacle of power, but debilitating humility was not one of TR's problems. Roosevelt tore into the presidency like a man who had won his own landslide, bringing a new mandate with him. Hanna and the rest of the McKinley machine then fully understood why their New York counterparts had been so eager to fob off their governor the year before.

No topic was too large or too small to escape Roosevelt's interest, from the rules of college football to a miners' strike in the anthracite coalfields of eastern Pennsylvania. Every president would like to dictate to Congress, but Roosevelt took it literally, piling pages of proposed legislation on the heads of his fellow Republicans at the other end of Pennsylvania Avenue. And much of what the accidental president wanted alarmed the big-business interests backing the GOP.

It got so bad that the Hanna faction was looking to scare up a primary challenge to Roosevelt in 1904, possibly even from one of the party's rising stars, William Howard Taft, who was just back from a stint as governor-general of the Philippines. Taft rebuffed the overture. And anyway, Hanna died that February, leaving Roosevelt the master and commander of his party.

That status was only enhanced when Roosevelt went on to smash Democrat Alton Parker in November. Roosevelt would win a full term by an even wider margin than McKinley had won reelection four years before.

Roosevelt was in command in a way that few presidents of his era would be. And one of his paramount concerns was the social change roiling a rapidly expanding nation. He meant to tame it and control it through progressive policies.

His reelection campaign had centered on his Square Deal platform—"All I ask is a square deal for every man. Give him a fair chance. Do not let him wrong any one, and do not let him be wronged." The goal was to go beyond the previous Republican ideal of equality in the eyes of the law. Roosevelt wanted nothing less than equality of opportunity for every American.

The idea may sound more than a little naïve after more than a century in which successive attempts to realize this goal by different names have failed to overcome deeply entrenched disadvantages of birth and circumstance for millions of Americans.

But in those days it sounded pretty radical, especially coming from an eastern Republican. Roosevelt, though, would insist that his version of progressive populism was practically minded compared to that of populist Democrats, and urgently needed in the face of huge social changes taking place.

The U.S. population increased by 46 percent between 1890 and 1910, from about 63 million to about 92 million. That is almost exactly double the growth rate from 1990 to 2010, when the population grew from 250 million to about 309 million.

Much of the boom of Roosevelt's era was a result of high birth rates, but the surge of immigration a century ago dwarfs anything we are familiar with today. Starting in 1905, an average of a million newcomers a year were pouring through the Ellis Island immigration station, just one of many ports of entry.

Like the immigrant waves that came before them, this one was greeted with alarm, particularly because these immigrants were predominantly from Southern and Eastern Europe. Roman Catholic, Eastern Orthodox, and Jewish immigrants were deemed too different from the dominant American culture to ever truly assimilate.

A particular area of concern was that these immigrants

would bring with them radical ideas like the ones that were sparking revolutions abroad.

When Czolgosz, the son of Polish Catholic immigrants and an avowed anarchist, killed McKinley, it was a manifestation of the worst fears of not just nativists, but the broad political establishment.

It is no surprise, then, that Roosevelt would make the suppression of anarchy one of the defining causes of the presidency he inherited, declaring years later that "when compared with the suppression of anarchy, every other question sinks into insignificance."

These were the turbulent social trends that Roosevelt wanted the government to master not just by law enforcement but also by remaking the system to deny anarchists and radicals causes with which to recruit new members and sow discord.

Republicans' post–Civil War success had left the party with a quandary. McKinley and his political sensei Hanna had forged a coalition that absorbed a booming merchant class and those working men who were finding increasing prosperity, but, thanks to support for protectionist tariffs, still managed to keep the support of the moneyed elite.

Tensions, however, were not far below the surface.

German immigrants of the mid-to-late nineteenth century may constitute the only identifiably Republican immigrant group in American history. That the party traces its birthplace to Ripon, Wisconsin, right in the heart of the Bratwurst Belt, stands as testament to that.

Lutheran and Roman Catholic German immigrants alike

gravitated toward and shaped the ethos of the party that was founded in the ashes of the Whigs.

From the beginning, Republicans' moral message of abolition, or at least opposition to the expansion of slavery, resonated with Germans driven from their homeland by religious and cultural strife. But the party's embrace from the start of pro-business policies did not hurt either, especially with those burghers who were finding increasing prosperity in cities like Milwaukee, Chicago, and, most definitely, the powerhouse GOP city of the day, Cincinnati.

By and large, this new energy was quite compatible with the remnants of the Whigs, who themselves were the remnants of the Federalists. Economic freedom and limited government are always popular with people who have money and feel like they have the means by which to control, or at least affect, the system.

But wave migration was not the only demographic upheaval taking place. A maturing industrial revolution was swiftly transforming the United States from a rural-agrarian nation to an urban one focused on manufacturing.

And here was where the rift between the conservative Republicans and the populists would erupt. Out in Wisconsin and other Republican strongholds of the Midwest, those German burghers and their farmer neighbors had serious concerns about the dominance of industrial interests in the east. Roosevelt's "trust busting" efforts to break up monopolies as president had been very popular with the growing progressive movement.

Your high school history teacher probably told you that

Roosevelt embraced populist, progressive workplace regulations after reading Upton Sinclair's 1906 novel *The Jungle* about the conditions in a Chicago meatpacking plant. Popular reception of the stomach-churning book certainly may have helped motivate Roosevelt, but he was no fan of muckrakers like Sinclair.

Less than two months after the book's publication, Roosevelt would use the occasion of laying the cornerstone for the new House Office Building, later to be named in honor of former House Speaker Joseph Cannon, to rail against "the man with the muck rake." He did not mention Sinclair by name, but the context is unmistakable:

Any excess is almost sure to invite a reaction; and, unfortunately, the reactions instead of taking the form of punishment of those guilty of the excess, is apt to take the form either of punishment of the unoffending or of giving immunity, and even strength, to offenders. The effort to make financial or political profit out of the destruction of character can only result in public calamity. Gross and reckless assaults on character, whether on the stump or in newspaper, magazine, or book, create a morbid and vicious public sentiment, and at the same time act as a profound deterrent to able men of normal sensitiveness and tend to prevent them from entering the public service at any price.

Roosevelt's urgent message for his party and for the political establishment—the "men of normal sensitiveness"—was to deprive the muckrakers of legitimate claims in order to protect what Roosevelt felt was good and decent about American republicanism and capitalism.

Republicans and capitalists may have seen it differently, but with Roosevelt having promised to not seek a third term, they were content to bide their time. Roosevelt, for his part, was content in the belief that his friend and loyal supporter Taft would carry on the work the Rough Rider had begun.

Roosevelt had used his position as the heir to a fortune and membership in a powerful family to shake the political establishment to its foundations. Taft, on the other hand, was an establishmentarian to his core.

Taft's father, Alphonso, had certainly benefited by his association with fellow Ohioan Ulysses Grant, serving as Grant's secretary of war and attorney general. Where Roosevelt had ducked the family business, the younger Taft very deliberately followed in his father's footsteps, attending Yale University before returning to Cincinnati for law school and embarking on an impressively solid career as a lawyer and judge.

The same Ohio faction that had helped his father eventually helped the younger Taft rise to become solicitor general under President Benjamin Harrison, arguing cases before the very Supreme Court to which the thirty-two-year-old lawyer dreamed of appointment.

Through this post and his impressive record there, Taft not only gained entree to the Washington political and cultural elite, but swiftly won himself an appointment to the new federal appellate court in Cincinnati.

Hoping that his supreme ambition was at hand, Taft eagerly responded to an invitation to meet with McKinley in 1900, but was instead tasked by the president with establishing civilian rule in what was then the American military governorship of the Philippines.

Taft's success in Manila outstripped expectations, including his own. When Roosevelt replaced McKinley, he eagerly advanced Taft, with whom he had crossed paths many times during their respective rises through Republican politics.

Roosevelt even offered Taft his dream job on the high court, a move that may have been at least somewhat self-interested on Roosevelt's part, as it would have eliminated a possible primary challenger for 1904. But an evidently agonizing Taft felt obliged to refuse for the sake of completing his duty in the Philippines.

Roosevelt, who had said of Taft for his Philippines service that "there is not in this Nation a higher or finer type of public servant," instead ended up elevating Taft to secretary of war after his duty in Manila was done.

While Colonel Roosevelt was quite content to conduct his own military policies—including even the exercise regimen for cadets at the service academies—he came to rely on Taft for advice on so much more.

After his 1905 inauguration, Roosevelt embarked on a two-month vacation in the Rockies and Southwest. Today's political press creates a clamor when a sitting president takes even a week at the beach with his family. Just imagine how reporters would react today to a president spending two months skylarking, including a week hunting wolves in Oklahoma and three weeks killing bear in Colorado.

Reporters at the time did wonder whether all of Roosevelt's pot-boiling policies—foreign and domestic—would need attention in his absence. "Oh, things will be all right," a departing Roosevelt told reporters. "I have left Taft sitting on the lid."

Secretary of State John Hay was abroad trying to recuperate from the worsening heart disease that would claim him the next year. Vice President Charles Fairbanks was a political and ideological enemy of Roosevelt's, foisted on TR at the 1904 convention.

That left Taft, ever dutiful and ever able, to function as acting president in Roosevelt's absence. In some ways, it was as if Roosevelt had never left. And that was exactly the kind of arrangement the president had in mind three years later when he put Taft forward as his designated successor.

With good reason. Taft had been willing to carry the fight for federal oversight of railroads to the recalcitrant Senate conservatives and their patrons in the industry—which Taft declared to be a "public institution"—with such progressive zeal that Roosevelt told reporters it "could not have been better expressed."

And when Taft initially balked at Roosevelt's offer of a soon-to-be-available seat on the Supreme Court in 1906, citing his family's urging that he keep his future political options open, TR knew he had his man. The president kept Taft on the campaign trail throughout the midterm race, a warm-up for the campaign to come.

Having a designated successor became more important to Roosevelt as Congress began to treat him as a lame duck. Having forsworn a third term, Roosevelt needed the credible threat of a Taft presidency to keep conservatives in Congress from open revolt.

Almost immediately, Roosevelt became frustrated by what he saw as Taft's laggardly approach to politics. Having generated a "boom" for his secretary of war, TR now saw the possibility of a backlash that could hand the nomination to a conservative candidate in 1908.

Or, maybe, Roosevelt being Roosevelt, he was thinking about himself. As 1907 progressed, public speculation began to grow that maybe TR would seek a third term after all. Only after that year's massive financial panic, which was laid at the feet of Roosevelt-designed restrictions on business and finance, was the president moved to reiterate his pledge not to run again. It would have to be up to Taft.

With Roosevelt back on board and the economy evening out, Taft saw his electoral fortunes quickly improve. While the Republican nomination was not assured, it was, with Roosevelt acting as de facto campaign manager and emotional crutch for the self-doubting front-runner, nearly in the bag.

Things were looking better for Taft, but worse for Roosevelt's agenda in Congress. For a second straight year, conservatives had managed to keep Roosevelt's progressive proposals bottled up. This only increased the urgency and anxiety Roosevelt felt about Taft's campaign.

Right up until the end, though, it was Roosevelt who was

causing the most political trouble for his designated successor. He spoke glumly to aides and friends about leaving office, and there was increasing chatter among the delegates that there might be a "stampede" for him.

Despite a couple of startles, though, Taft came through, the unanimous choice on the first ballot, and grateful heir to the Roosevelt mantle. As the fall election hove into view, he was increasingly criticized for appearing to be a Roosevelt lackey and not his own man.

He carried the draft of his campaign kickoff speech to Roosevelt at Oyster Bay, New York, seeking the incumbent's approval, and, against Roosevelt's advice, opened the speech with a paean to the president.

But for all the talk of Taft as a weakling, Roosevelt and reporters should perhaps have paid more attention to what came next in the speech. "The chief function of the next administration is distinct from, and a progressive development of, that which has been performed by President Roosevelt," Taft told the crowd in Cincinnati. "The chief function of the next Administration is to complete and perfect the machinery by which these standards may be maintained."

Taft, who had cultivated the image of an unwilling politician, was intentionally describing his ambition to be a caretaker president when what Roosevelt really wanted was a proxy to carry on his fight against conservatives in Congress.

Luckily for Taft, Democrats had fallen back into bad habits and gave William Jennings Bryan his third nomination, perhaps because of the agitation caused by the panic in the previous year, or perhaps just for old times' sake. Whatever the cause, Bryan's radical platform and antiquated ways offered Taft a wide berth to an easy Electoral College win.

The first stirrings of the coming rift between Taft and Roosevelt came as the president-elect was putting together his cabinet, preferring to replace key Roosevelt allies with his own men.

Roosevelt shrugged it off, and in their last friendly correspondence the two men heaped praise upon each other, with Roosevelt gushing, "Nice isn't anything like a strong enough word, but at the moment to use words as strong as I feel would look sloppy." The hearts-for-eyes emoji of the day...

The outgoing president left Congress and his successor with a twenty-one-thousand-word bill of particulars that Roosevelt expected to be carried out in his absence. The to-do list was not just voluminously worded, but voluminous in scope. Roosevelt demanded action on education, social welfare, trade regulations, government finances, foreign affairs, national defense, and everything else that the still-young president had left undone.

Republicans were instructed not only to cement the changes to business regulations that Roosevelt had championed, but also to enact welfare programs and other initiatives that would help the burgeoning working class "get their fair share of the benefit of business prosperity."

Courts, however, frowned upon these progressive innovations, with judges at the state and federal levels deciding that

Roosevelt's activist agenda could not fit in the confines of the Constitution. And Taft, ever the lawyer, happened to agree.

Your high school history teacher probably also summed up the terrible rift in the Republican Party of 1912 and that tumultuous Chicago convention as being about personal animosity between Roosevelt and Taft. And to be sure, the enmity was real. As historian Lewis Gould neatly juxtaposed, "Taft declared Roosevelt to be 'the greatest menace to our institutions that we have had in a long time.' Roosevelt saw Taft as the agent of 'the forces of reaction and of political crookedness.'"

So it's not like they were making friendship bracelets for each other. But the maelstrom of 1912 had been in the works since long before Roosevelt ever got astride a charging Bull Moose. The fight between the progressive populists and the conservatives was coming with or without TR and Taft.

A fight over tariffs exacerbated the rift between the warring wings of the party and helped Democrats to eventually retake the House in 1910 for the first time in sixteen years.

While Taft had been presiding over the diminution of Republican prospects in Washington, Roosevelt was busy on a yearlong trip across Africa and Europe. He treated his safari like he treated politics: with unabashed bloodlust. He and his large party killed thousands of animals in Africa for the purported benefit of the Smithsonian Institution and the American Museum of Natural History.

Though he tried to appear aloof from politics on his travels, by the time Roosevelt made it to Europe he was expressing growing concern to friends like Gifford Pinchot, who had been forced out as head of the Forest Service under the Taft administration.

By the time Roosevelt came home in the summer of 1910, he was ready for full rupture with the man he had once considered a loyal apostle. In August of that year, he traveled to Osawatomie, Kansas, to deliver the speech that would mark not just the rift between the two men, but the battle for the soul of the GOP.

Roosevelt laid out the doctrine of "new nationalism," and it was bold even by his standards. The progressive agenda included many long-held desires of the movement, including the direct election of senators; women's suffrage; an income tax; a minimum wage; welfare programs for the aged, unemployed, and disabled; and even a national health service.

It was the kind of Prairie Populism that Bryan had been preaching in the other party for decades. Roosevelt even suggested that the conservative policies of the day were tantamount to slavery.

"The essence of any struggle for healthy liberty has always been, and must always be, to take from some one man or class of men the right to enjoy power, or wealth, or position, or immunity, which has not been earned by service to his or their fellows," he said. "That is what you fought for in the Civil War, and that is what we strive for now."

Government, he argued, should allow citizens to gain wealth "only so long as the gaining represents benefit to the community."

Where Roosevelt had once argued for progressive reforms because the system had to bend in order to not break amid sweeping societal change, he was now arguing for progressivism for its own sake.

Roosevelt summoned progressives out of the Populist Party as well as those on the Democratic side to join him and his fellow Republican progressives in taking over the party. Taft rightly perceived this declaration of political war by his former mentor as an existential threat, not just to his presidency, but to the party he and his family had loved and served since its birth. From that moment forward, Taft and other former friends of Roosevelt began bracing for the coming storm of 1912.

Roosevelt took to lambasting Taft with characteristic gusto, mocking as he went. Taft, with characteristic calculation, started laying a trap for his old boss.

By the time their respective factions would converge in Chicago in the summer of 1912, it was open warfare, and not just in a figurative sense. Fistfights punctuated rallies and the level of invective reached such a point that even the pugilistic Roosevelt felt obliged to tell his loyal army of supporters to dial it back.

Roosevelt was counting on the energies of the growing American Midwest and West, particularly in larger cities. But Taft had control of the party apparatus.

And perhaps best for Taft was that Roosevelt chose dangerous ground on which to contest the nomination. Speaking in Columbus, Ohio, in February 1912, Roosevelt laid out what would become his platform, including advocacy for "pure

Democracy." That would have been enough to rankle Republicans. But then Roosevelt took it another step further and focused his anger on the judiciary that had been so assiduously cutting down his legacy since he left office.

He proposed that judicial decisions should be subject to recall by voters. This proved a breaking point for longtime Roosevelt friends and supporters like Henry Cabot Lodge, who publicly denounced the proposal despite his longstanding friendship with TR.

By the end of that month when Roosevelt declared himself officially a candidate, the former president may have been surging in popular support, but his party was hardening its defenses against the onslaught.

Fortunately for Taft, who dreaded the idea of campaigning as a sitting president, Roosevelt's assault on the judiciary gave the incumbent just the right topic. He had finally found his voice in defending the institution he loved.

It's important here to understand how Taft and his fellow Republicans were evolving in their thinking through this struggle. Taft had become convinced that Roosevelt truly was a danger to the country, and realized that if he succeeded in frustrating Roosevelt's efforts to grab the nomination, TR and his supporters would bolt the party.

Roosevelt had been racking up popular support with his pugnacious oratory, particularly aimed at a corrupt, self-serving judicial system that he said had become a tool of oppression "fundamentally hostile to every species of real popular government."

The state conventions of that year were frequently marked with violence. The *New York Times* reported how Michigan militiamen had intervened at that state's convention and "restored order with their clubs." Similar scenes played out in Missouri, Oklahoma, and elsewhere.

A pattern emerged through the spring in which the Roosevelt faction carried the day in directly elected primaries while Team Taft prevailed at conventions dominated by party bosses. Even when the progressives lost, though, they would still gather separately and choose their own slates of delegates, declaring the proceedings to be rigged.

Neither faction would come to Chicago with enough delegates to win on the first ballot, but Roosevelt was intent on getting additional progressive delegates seated from the contested state results. And party leaders feared that the same violence that had marred state-level proceedings would play out in Chicago.

The first fight was over which delegates to seat. But the Taft faction managed to get former secretary of state Elihu Root installed as temporary chairman, albeit narrowly. This would be, upon reflection, a death blow for Roosevelt's chances. Not one to take a setback in stride, Roosevelt took the unusual step of going to Chicago himself, rallying his supporters and directing their at least figurative effort to overrun the establishment.

Taft, meanwhile, affected an air of executive remove from the proceedings, dividing his time between official duties and rounds of golf, but all the while hanging on every telegram and phone call from his team in Chicago, where the mood remained ominous.

The violence of the winter and spring and the growing menace in Chicago had helped turn Taft, and many other Roosevelt men, not just against their onetime leader, but also against many of the ideas upon which they had previously agreed. The Republican experiment with progressivism was drawing to a close, even as it seemed to be reaching its pinnacle.

Taft explained his choice in a letter to a friend, writing that should Roosevelt make good on his threat to leave the party, the president vowed to "retain the regular organization of the party as a nucleus about which the conservative people who are in favor of maintaining constitutional government can gather."

He felt it would be better for Republicans to preserve their party's principles in a defeat at the hands of Democrats than see populists overrun the GOP.

Serious violence never materialized in Chicago, but Roosevelt's threat to leave his party did come to pass. The former president gathered his supporters across town after Taft was declared the winner on a narrow first-ballot vote.

The Progressive Party was born on the night of June 22, 1912, at Orchestra Hall, where Roosevelt declared to the disaffected delegates, "If you wish me to make the fight I will make it, even if only one state should support me."

Former New York senator Chauncey Depew probably said it best as both conventions came to a close: "The only question now is which corpse gets the most flowers."

Depew was right. Democrats had a spirited and sometimes

contentious convention the next week in Baltimore, but settled on New Jersey governor Woodrow Wilson without the bitter acrimony that had afflicted Republicans.

Wilson would go on to win easily with just 42 percent of the popular vote but forty of forty-eight states.

The final tally would seem to have suggested that Roosevelt's new party, which won six states compared to just two for Republicans, was the better bet for the future. The Progressives had won rapidly growing California and Michigan and performed better in urban areas.

But just four years later, the Progressives were kaput. Wilson and the Democrats had enacted or at least embraced much of Roosevelt's platform, while Republicans had recovered dramatically in the 1914 midterm elections. And with Europe at war, dramatic experiments in domestic policy perhaps sounded too risky.

By 1920, Republicans not only had retaken the White House, but also obtained their largest majorities in Congress since Reconstruction. Even Roosevelt had rejoined the GOP, shunning the nomination of the new party he founded just four years before.

Taft's gamble had paid off.

Roosevelt set out to remake the Republican Party, and there's no doubt he did—twice: first, as an exuberant, accidental president who shoved the GOP out of the Gilded Age; and second, as the cause of a counterrevolution.

The conservative, pro-business, limited-government Republican Party America would know for generations to come was in considerable part born in the reaction to Roosevelt's assault of 1912. The swing of every policeman's club at a state convention riot was a hammer blow shutting the door on the party's openness to progressivism.

So how did someone who seemed to have his finger on the political pulse of his country and his party fall to pieces so quickly?

It has been said that the secret to success in politics is like being the baton major at the head of a marching band. You're not really leading the parade, you just happen to be in front of it. One of the dangers for populist leaders is to misunderstand that relationship.

And if you happen to be part of the ruling caste, like TR, it is even easier to get confused. Are you using your position on behalf of those without lofty station, or are you creating the movement yourself?

The secret for any successful populist is to swing the baton like you mean it but never forget that the parade will go on without you.

CHAPTER FOUR

Foolishness

(For Good and for Ill)

In the summer of 1935, Huey Long was a sensation.

The gentleman from Louisiana had been a hit with the Washington press corps since the moment he arrived in the Senate in 1932. Long had actually won the seat in 1930, but he left it vacant for more than a year so he could remain governor long enough to smite the last of his political enemies back home.

In fact, the 1930 campaign had been an improvisation. Long was stymied by a state legislature that was growing less afraid of his political power. So the governor used his smashing victory in the Senate run as a show of political strength.

And while he surely was popular, Long wasn't taking any chances on how smashing his victory would be. Long historian Richard White wrote that in one parish "the official record indicated that voters marched to the polls in alphabetical order."

When Huey Pierce Long smote you, he expected you to stay smote.

But now Long had a problem. Unlike Lyndon Johnson, who had the foresight to ram through a law in Texas letting him seek two federal offices simultaneously ahead of his 1960 vice presidential run, Long was going to have to choose. The Senate win had proven his clout, yes, but it meant that he was going to have to give up the governorship that made him "the Kingfish."

The fight was a wild one. At one point Long even dispatched the state's National Guard to cordon off the capitol and governor's mansion from his own lieutenant governor to keep him from taking power. Eventually, though, Long got a more obedient crony set up as the new lieutenant governor and had another devotee ready to run with the backing of the Long machine when the term ended in 1932.

Satisfied that he would retain power of the governorship if not the title of governor, Long finally was ready to head to Washington.

He made up for lost time and quickly figured out his new national audience. Reporters stuck in Senate hearings and debates, then as now, always gobble up good copy. And the man they dubbed, in a groaner among all groaners, the "Terror of the Bayous" dished it out.

From the tips of his gangster-chic two-tone spectator shoes to the straw boater hat perched atop his well-oiled locks, Long was a thirty-nine-year-old walking, talking outrage generation machine.

Long insulted his enemies with deadly accuracy and unusual coarseness. A Louisiana politician who opposed his agenda and who was known to have gastrointestinal troubles was dubbed "Whistle Britches." Long called the Constitutional League that was formed to oppose his many, many usurpations "the Constipational League." Whatever else Long was, he was funny as hell.

He also knew one of the first rules for getting coverage in Washington: Bash your own team. Long savagely attacked his own party, blocking Democratic measures with his famous filibusters. If Americans knew well enough what a filibuster was for one to be the centerpiece of *Mr. Smith Goes to Washington* in 1939, Frank Capra could thank Long.

Long eventually resigned all his committee appointments in protest of Majority Leader Joe Robinson, who Long said was a crook in the employ of his former corporate clients. Robinson's real mistake was trying to outdo Long. The Democratic leader quickly found himself out-demagogued by maybe the best in American history.

Remember that these were the days when Robinson was considered a bit of a wild man for his table-pounding, stentorian oratory. Long, a student of both Baptist preaching and his state-championship high school debate team, would not be outdone by some Arkansas Methodist.

Long wasn't a good speaker in any traditional sense. Slashing his arms like a wind-up soldier and bleating like a shoat, he managed to simultaneously preserve both the air of a man in a hurry to get someplace important and a man on the run. But he slashed and bleated with unnatural force. And with an almost superhuman memory he was able to marshal facts and figures (some of which were actually true) in his service.

Put all that together with his homey jokes and putdowns and you had the most fearsome orator of his day.

"A mob is coming here in six months to hang the other ninety-five of you damned scoundrels," Long told his fellow senators in one of his floor speech doozies, "and I'm undecided whether to stick here with you or go out and lead them."

Long also quickly learned to flatter, wheedle, and threaten reporters in Washington, just as he had done in Baton Rouge. And they were surely smitten. Even as the *Washington Post* was calling for his expulsion five months after he arrived, the paper's news columns couldn't get enough of the hot copy. Call it clickbait, Depression-era style.

Sam Jones, who in 1940 would become the first governor to knock the Longite faction out after a dozen years in absolute power, declared, "More bunkum has been written about Huey Long and his place in history than any man in this region I know of."

That may be so. But save a little sympathy for the reporters. Long definitely knew his target audience. One Louisiana newspaperman recalled to the *New Yorker* that in Prohibition days, Long had been known to drop off favorable press clippings at the reporter's home with a half gallon of moonshine, just in case the verbiage wasn't enough to get him stoned.

By the summer of 1935, Long found himself in a precarious place between punch line and public enemy. His outlandish lines were getting plenty of press, but he didn't have the kind of national clout he needed to make moves in Washington like he did in Baton Rouge. But at the same time, the establishment wasn't laughing anymore.

One of President Franklin Roosevelt's advisers recalled FDR saying, "It's all very well for us to laugh over Huey, but he really is one of the two most dangerous men in the country."

(The other was said to be then–major general Douglas

MacArthur, who had won the love of populists on the oppo-
site end of the political spectrum from Long. MacArthur used
tanks and tear gas to drive an encampment of World War I
veterans out of Washington. The members of the Bonus Army
were militating for early payment of their service bonuses, and
some on the right considered them incipient communists.)

It's a matter of debate whether Long really intended to
challenge Roosevelt in 1936 or if he was feinting to gener-
ate support and organization for a 1940 race. When in doubt
about Long's motives, I tend to come down on the side of rank
opportunism. I doubt he had any idea that he would come so
far, so fast, and I suspect he was just playing out the string to
see where it took him.

Long's national celebrity had been growing since February
1934 when NBC had given him a national platform to broadcast what would become his most famous speech, "Every Man
a King."

Long borrowed the line from William Jennings Bryan,
whom he admired and emulated (except in his personal and
professional conduct). Facing impeachment for corruption
and indecency (yep and yep) less than a year into his first term
as governor, Long distributed flyers—at taxpayer expense, of
course—that cast his troubles as an effort by Standard Oil to
preserve its profits. The headline: "The Cross of Gold: Standard Oil Company vs. Huey P. Long."

NBC knew that it had a hit on its hands with Long, for
whom the network furnished regular broadcasts after the
blockbuster success of his first speech. NBC bragged that it

received more than sixty thousand letters from listeners in response to Long's speeches, and Long said that tens of thousands more flooded his Senate office.

Long claimed in the spring of 1935 that more than seven million people had joined the almost thirty thousand local Share Our Wealth clubs he was hawking on air, a pretty impressive start for his presumed primary challenge of Roosevelt the next year.

H. L. Mencken, the misanthropic antipopulist of the day, called Long a "backwoods demagogue of the oldest and most familiar model—impudent, blackguardly, and infinitely prehensile." What Mencken also knew, though, was that many of his fellow Americans thought those were entirely reasonable responses to the moment.

Certainly the span between the assassination of John F. Kennedy in Dealey Plaza on November 22, 1963, and the final helicopter taking off from the roof of the American embassy in Saigon on April 30, 1975, makes its claim for the era of deepest national disquiet since the Civil War. It was certainly far worse than our current period's disheartening blend of government incapacity and authoritarianism.

But trust me when I say that what was happening in the country when Long was executing his designs on the republic was far more disturbing. The period between the start of the Great Depression and the turning of the tide in World War II in 1942 was the moment of greatest danger to our system since Fort Sumter.

For three generations we have been playing with house money, enjoying the dividends of the Pax Americana. But eighty-three years ago, rebelling against the establishment meant something different. Americans today are having a pretty vigorous discussion about whether capitalism and republicanism are still working. But in the mid-1930s, there was a far better argument to say that they were not.

The Depression was heading into a painful second dip and Long was hardly the only voice calling for a radical departure from American norms.

Progressives had been arguing since before Woodrow Wilson ran in 1912 that a government of constitutionally limited powers was too slow, too antiquated, and too weak to meet the needs of modernity. As the dark decade of the 1930s trudged on, more Americans on the political right were starting to agree.

The Nazi enthusiasts of the German American Bund claimed two hundred thousand members; and luminaries like Henry Ford, Charles Lindbergh, and Joseph Kennedy expressed admiration for the pseudoscientific pragmatism of European fascism.

Many of the same folks who admired MacArthur for rolling tanks on a shanty village by the banks of the Potomac thought that maybe we needed a generalissimo here—that liberty was simply not suited to either the chaos or the efficiency of the modern era.

A consensus between voices on the right and left was

starting to emerge that a system arranged around protecting individual liberties was no longer sustainable. The disagreement was over what to replace it with.

It was not quite clear to anyone, Long included, exactly what his alternative system was. Step one was to install Long as ruler, step two was to confiscate all fortunes of more than $8 million for redistribution among the poor, and step three... well, we'd just have to sort that out later.

"Every man a king," Long said, "so there would be no such thing as a man or woman who did not have the necessities of life who would not be dependent upon the whims and caprices and ipse dixit of the financial barons for a living."

Long surely knew he was mostly ipse dixit—assertions made but not proved—himself. But he also understood the awesome power of the new mass medium of radio, especially for blunt, simple ideas.

And there could hardly be anything more blunt or simple than the idea that powerful elites were denying desperate Americans access to a simple, permanent solution to their many woes. If populism was a church, Long would have been its greatest ever preacher of the prosperity gospel.

Free money, it turns out, has always been pretty popular.

All this speechifying meant lots of trips to New York for broadcasts. By then, though, Long had skimmed enough money off of his awesome graft machine still humming along in Baton Rouge that he could travel in style. He was worth something like $2 million, having taken his share of the wealth first.

When he was in town, he set himself up at the new Hotel

New Yorker, where he would hold court with reporters and his many admirers. It was also the scene of one of his greatest publicity stunts.

For all the pleasures that Manhattan had to offer, it could not produce one of Long's greatest delights from home: the Ramos gin fizz. When he was in New Orleans, Long kept his quarters at the Roosevelt Hotel. Its Sazerac Bar was his throne room, and a Ramos gin fizz was his scepter. But he could not find anything like its equal in post-Prohibition New York.

Basic gin fizzes are just gin, citrus, simple syrup, and soda water, but the Ramos version is a souped-up, sickly sweet froth that adds orange flower water, milk, powdered sugar, and egg white. Shaken until the bartender's hands ache from the cold, the drink is served in a fat flute or a tumbler.

It looks like a chemistry experiment gone awry, smells like your grandmother's perfume, and tastes like a Creamsicle. Long, of course, adored them.

His remedy for the uninspiring Ramos fizzes at the Hotel New Yorker was perfectly Longian: grandiose, self-serving, and paid for by someone else. He called the manager at the Roosevelt Hotel, Seymour Weiss, and told him to dispatch head bartender Sam Guarino to New York—at taxpayer expense, of course—to put on a clinic.

Then Long rounded up a press conference, complete with newsreel cameras, to take in the spectacle, which was not exactly a heavy lift. If you can't get reporters to a bar on a hot New York summer day with the promise of free booze and easy copy, you're not even trying.

Long railed against FDR, mugged for the cameras, concocted a perfectly phony story about how his grandfather was the true inventor of the Ramos gin fizz, and generally made a spectacle of himself.

The *Times* took an approach far drier than the drink in its description of the scene: "After some more posing for photographers and the talkies—the whole performance consumed fully an hour—the Kingfish left the bar with a broad grin, leading a crowd of reporters to his apartment on the 22nd floor of the hotel, where he spent two hours discoursing on the political situation."

Just as an aside here, imagine the response today if a U.S. senator and likely presidential candidate hosted a gaggle of reporters for two hours of off-the-record tipsy talk in his luxury hotel room. One imagines that it would merit either more than a throwaway line in the story or absolutely no mention at all (until it leaked on Twitter).

If you can picture the senator there in his white double-breasted suit slinging frothed gin and frothier political attacks you will see why it is altogether right and fitting that among the jobs Long worked as a young man was a stint hawking patent medicine during the golden age of quackery.

Long's very first job, which came at about age thirteen, was selling books. It would be unkind of me to say that selling books in north-central Louisiana in 1908 would be like trying to sell umbrellas in the Sahara Desert, so I'll let Long tell it.

After the bookseller marveled at his ability to make sales in the intellectual desert of his youth, Long had an epiphany.

In William Ivy Hair's history, *The Kingfish and His Realm*, Long's success helped him realize, as he would later recall, "I can sell anybody anything."

But if selling books where illiteracy and poverty conspire to suppress learning is hard, then selling patent medicine to the same folks is only too easy.

Remember that this was back when Clark "Rattlesnake King" Stanley was still selling his snake oil liniment and medicine shows were in their prime, crisscrossing rural America peddling miracle cures and playing hillbilly music. This was all before radio shows and pure food and drug laws ruined the racket—back when there was still a little cocaine in your great-grandmother's Coca-Cola.

Long started selling McElree's Wine of Cardui, a potion produced by the Chattanooga Medicine Company that promised "women's relief." The label of a bottle from Long's era declares, "For menstrual disturbances of women...falling of the womb, change of life, and as a general restorative for delicate women."

Contemporary newspaper advertisements further promised that "taken at the proper time," Wine of Cardui also "relieves pain, corrects derangements, quiets nervousness."

No wonder it sold so well. Who among us wouldn't want their derangements corrected?

Long was selling for one of the biggest names in the field, the Chattanooga Medicine Company—the moneymaking brainchild of a couple of carpetbaggers. The company did its best business with Wine of Cardui and a laxative called Black Draught that users found, if anything, too effective.

That's not to say that Cardui didn't have an effect. The stuff was 20 percent alcohol with various thistles, herbs, and bark in the extract. If some 40-proof wine doesn't calm your nerves then nothing would.

Eventually, though, the crusaders at the American Medical Association would come after Cardui with articles pointing out the "vicious fraud" of promising desperate women that it would reverse infertility. And once the feds started controlling controlled substances, nostrums that relied on drink or dope were banned.

(Chattanooga Medicine, by the way, would eventually go straight, change its name to Chattem, and make products you know like Icy Hot, Dexatrim, Rolaids, and, naturally, Pamprin to treat pain, reduce bloating, and "relieve irritability" among women suffering with menstrual discomfort.)

Rackets as good as Wine of Cardui can't go on forever. But while the government can outlaw scam medicines, it will never stop scam politics. After all, if they started keeping scam artists out of government, they'd never be able to get a quorum in Congress.

And Long knew that his salesmanship was meant for bigger things than hustling herbal hooch to the menopausal women of Winn Parish. He had also learned a secret that every good con man knows: You can't really swindle a truly honest man.

A well-worn story in my family holds that a hundred years ago or so in southern Illinois, my great-grandfather's best horse was struck by lightning as he was cresting a rise on the way home from Greenup. When the insurance man came to settle the claim, he asked James Stirewalt to sign on the line swearing that he had seen the horse killed by lightning. Old Jim refused.

My great-grandfather was not going to be tricked into telling a lie by a fast-talking insurance man. That horse could have had a heart attack or coincidentally expired of natural causes, so that bitterly poor man barely feeding his three children on a fifteen-acre patch left the money on the table. He might have been a fool, but he was determined to be an honest one.

We recount the story in my family today as a caution against pridefulness, but what made it stick in the mind of his son, my grandfather, was how desperately they needed that money. I doubt many would have faulted old Jim if he would have out-and-out scammed the insurance company.

Oppression of any kind makes people desperate, and there are few kinds of oppression as complete and permeating as poverty. Long came from a family that at least by comparison to his desperately poor neighbors was educated and comfortable. But as he would later say, he knew well "the desperate stare" in the eyes of the poor.

We like to think of power and wealth as the great corrupting forces, and they can be, but want corrupts just as powerfully, if not more so. Virtues can quickly come to look like luxury items. And as British politician and political philosopher Edmund Burke held, "All who have ever written on government are unanimous, that among a people generally corrupt, liberty cannot long exist."

Whether Long was selling patent medicine, gin fizzes, or

Share Our Wealth, he knew that the best marks were the ones who were desperate enough not just to be conned, but to do half of the work themselves. The most willing victims fill in the blanks spots for the con man, especially if it seems like the hustler is going places.

And that was all Long ever really wanted to do: be going somewhere else. Which stands to reason. Very few men or women alive today could conjure the isolation of the Winnfield, Louisiana, of Long's youth.

There were no telephones, no railroad station, and few visitors from the world beyond. The closest town of any size was Alexandria, a day's ride away—and that was only when the gully-washed roads were passable.

By the time Long was old enough to be selling door-to-door, trains were coming through. But it was mostly pinewood rolling on the Tremont and Gulf Railroad bound for the paper mills up near Monroe.

Winfield, by our hyperconnected standards, still feels like an isolated outpost. As your speedometer reaches 65 or 70 miles per hour and the ribbon of concrete under your tires starts producing a satisfying hum, it's easy to understand why Long was so pleased with his highway projects as governor. To escape those slash pines and that hard dome of a summer sky and feel fresh air in your face still feels like sweet release.

Long certainly despised the poverty and ignorance of his home place, but it was its isolation that seems to have driven him into a life aimed at sucking down every drop that he could wring out of it for himself.

If you ever wonder why corruption is so ruinous to republics, just meditate on Long for a minute.

His supporters, especially in Louisiana, had ample evidence that the game was rigged squarely against them. Standard Oil did get its way in the legislature. Schools and roads were in disgraceful condition outside of the larger cities. The New Orleans political machine did skim the cream off of the treasury for itself and its supporters.

Long's pitch, in essence, was that he may have been a bad guy, but he was their bad guy. When he kicked off his shoe during a speech to show the hole in his cotton sock wide enough to stick his big toe through, his audience knew he was one of them. And his promise of rough justice for their oppressors sounded pretty good.

When the elites howled about impropriety and unconstitutional conduct, Long said that it was not only evidence that his assault on the corrupt elites was working, but that those pieties were bogus all along. The rules were instruments of oppression, and that's why the Kingfish needed to break them.

That's a pretty nifty permission structure he built for himself, a wide boulevard through which could pass any number of misconducts. Graft, bribery, vote rigging, intimidation, and even physical violence carried out by henchmen could all be accommodated.

Some he defended outright, some he winked slyly at, and others he simply dismissed as the fabrications of the elites.

On one of Long's New York trips, he managed to make quite a drunken spectacle of himself at a charity dinner on

Long Island. Here's how anti-Long *Time* magazine described the scene:

> He sat down with strangers, made himself objection-able with vulgar greetings. Spotting a plump girl with a full plate before her, he marched to her table, snatched the plate from her, yapped: "You're too fat already. I'll eat this." He danced just once—until his partner's husband took the lady away. He thrust himself behind the bar, shoved its tender aside, loudly proclaimed that he would show the world how they mix and shake them in Louisiana.

Oh dear.

The episode ended with Long urinating on the trouser leg of another guest who refused to "make way for the Kingfish" at the urinals. The guest socked Long in the eye, causing the senator to take flight with a shiner already starting to well up.

What would he tell the folks back home about such a pitiful episode of him drunk, disorderly, and defeated?

By the time the story had found its way to New York newspapers, Long was already in Milwaukee to address the Veterans of Foreign Wars convention. Asked about his humiliation, he said in a press release that one of the many enemies of his programs had sent thugs to kill him:

> I saw one strike at my head with a knife or something sharp and I ducked just so that it grazed my forehead.

One man was blocking the door but I stumbled low through him and managed to wriggle clear. I felt blood coming down my face. We have tried to find out the persons who did the ganging.... I have been repeatedly threatened. I was lucky to have escaped and am grateful.

He was not a drunken boor, you see, but rather a martyr for the cause, bleeding for his fellow forgotten men and women.

Even if you knew he was a liar and a hustler, you might still enjoy the whole spectacle of the thing. Long's antics competed with the comics for the most entertaining part of every day's newspaper. He was, as I said, a sensation.

That's not entirely a bad thing, or maybe even a mostly bad thing. The best part about being a young country so thoroughly and completely blessed with land, resources, distance, and timing has been that it has allowed us to be foolish so often.

We have fallen for many silly fads over the generations. Americans love a good salesman, and our devotion to get-rich-quick schemes and miracle cures is evidence of gullibility, yes, but also of optimism. We may get suckered into shortcuts to El Dorado, but we still think there's a city of gold out there somewhere. Things generally do not end well for those who prey on such hopes, though. And so it was for Long.

He returned to Baton Rouge at the end of the long, hot summer of 1935 to reimpose himself on his subjects. He stayed late at the skyscraper statehouse he had built as a monument to himself. He was bossing through a legislative package designed, of course, to tighten his machine's grip on power by removing anti-Longite judge Benjamin Pavy from his post.

Walking out with his goon squad around him, Long was confronted by Pavy's son-in-law, twenty-eight-year-old Dr. Carl Weiss. Long had already discharged Weiss's in-laws from teaching jobs in public schools and even suggested that Weiss's wife was the illegitimate product of the judge's consorting with a mixed-race woman.

Weiss fired four shots at Long, whose bodyguards responded with a hail of bullets. When they picked up the dead doctor's body and the slugs fell out, one observer said that it sounded like someone had dropped a handful of gravel on the smooth marble floor.

Long held on for two days but, in a most fitting turn, died at the hands of an unqualified quack whom he had installed for patronage purposes as the official state physician.

There is an argument to be made that if Long hadn't been murdered he would have mounted a successful presidential run the next year. He had a clear brand as a populist Robin Hood, a grassroots organization (thanks to NBC radio and his Share Our Wealth clubs), and an electorate that was angry and anxious in the face of the second dip of the Great Depression.

Long is the subject of one of the best political novels ever written, Robert Penn Warren's *All the King's Men*. But the fictionalized version of Long in Warren's book, Willie Stark, isn't the kind of guy who could have given FDR trouble in 1936. Stark is a dangerous demagogue for sure, but he's too much a prisoner of his own venality and other base impulses to be a successful dictator. *All the King's Men* is more of a story about human frailty than anything else.

The book that tells the story of the Long that Roosevelt and others feared is Sinclair Lewis's 1935 *It Can't Happen Here*. In Lewis's version, the Long character is Berzelius "Buzz" Windrip. Windrip campaigns for president as a populist, defeats Roosevelt, and swiftly installs himself as dictator. It's a quasi-satire intended to make Americans alarmed by the rise of fascism in Europe understand that yes, it could happen here. Windrip, though, is not the kind of guy who urinates on trouser legs in men's rooms and shakes gin fizzes. Instead, he is a hillbilly Hitler, and just as deadly sincere—and delivers the same kind of deadly results.

It would be unfair to say that Long was insincere in his beliefs, but there's no doubt that both he and his audience were aware to a degree that there was a con going on.

Consider the nickname he embraced. The Kingfish was a character on the most popular program of the day, the radio minstrel show *Amos 'n' Andy*.

Amos and Andy were unwitting country boys from Georgia who were trying to navigate life in the big city of Chicago. And George Stevens was "the Kingfish" at the Mystic Knights of the Sea lodge. He used his position to trick and bully the unwitting protagonists into all sorts of trouble.

That Long would embrace a comparison to such a character is striking, but more striking was that his supporters would, too. They knew that Long was corrupt, dishonest, and in possession of a wide authoritarian streak. But they believed that he was one of them and was using his powers, at least sometimes, to get for them.

Did the women who bought patent medicine from Long as a young man believe that Wine of Cardui was a miracle cure? How many of them knew the racket and understood that it was a legal, societally acceptable way to buy booze? How many of them took very lightly the claims of the maker and its young salesman? How many enjoyed the medicine show or the sales pitch more than they liked the product?

America might have elected president a man who embraced his con-man status well enough to take the nickname of a hustler from a comedy series. If the Depression had gotten even deeper, if Roosevelt faltered, if the world hadn't been looking so ominous, anything might have been possible for a politician of Long's gifts. But to allow him to become a dictator?

Germany and Italy had weak institutions, little history of self-governance, and they had been ravaged by war in profoundly damaging ways. America, on the other hand, could afford a little foolishness.

Andrew Jackson may have been our first celebrity president. He was the first to have a biographical campaign book published and was highly protective of his image in the press. But it was this lithograph circulated by his political team depicting the Battle of New Orleans (1815) that put him in hundreds of thousands of homes across the country. Jackson's victory was a point of enormous pride in the young republic, and the advent of cheap lithography meant that ordinary Americans could display this fine piece of art in their homes... with Jackson at the center. *(Library of Congress)*

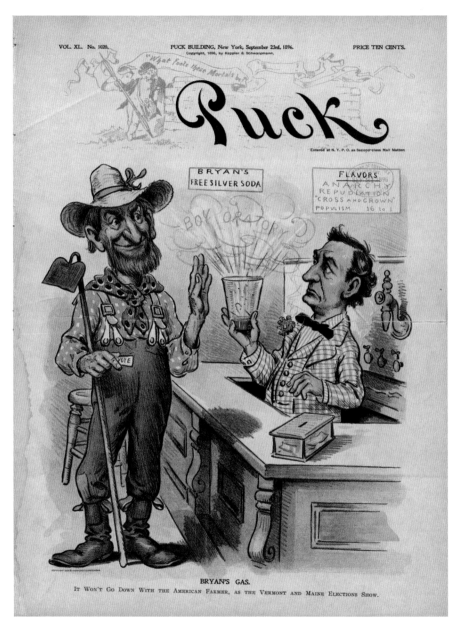

VOL. XL. No. 1020.   PUCK BUILDING, New York, September 23rd, 1896.   PRICE TEN CENTS.
Copyright, 1896, by Keppler & Schwarzmann.

Entered at N. Y. P. O. as Second-class Mail Matter.

BRYAN'S
FREE SILVER SODA

FLAVORS
ANARCHY
REPUDIATION
"CROSS AND CROWN"
POPULISM   16 to 1

BRYAN'S GAS.
IT WON'T GO DOWN WITH THE AMERICAN FARMER, AS THE VERMONT AND MAINE ELECTIONS SHOW.

Political cartoonist J.S. Pughe summed up the attitude of many in the East to William Jennings Bryan's surprising nomination at the 1896 Democratic National Convention. Bryan, then a thirty-six-year-old former two-term congressman from Nebraska, was an improbable choice. But *Puck* was wrong about how "Bryan's Gas" would go over with farmers. He took William McKinley down to the wire in November. His concoction was so appealing to Democrats that they couldn't help but nominate him two more times, though to increasingly poor effect. *(Library of Congress)*

In 1912, it was still considered unseemly for presidential candidates to appear at their own nominating conventions. But when the vote started turning against Teddy Roosevelt, the former president couldn't bear to stay away completely. He traveled to Chicago to rally his supporters after a procedural vote excluded Roosevelt delegates. This throng gathered outside of Roosevelt's hotel, where he exhorted: "Fearless of the future; unheeding of our individual fates; with unflinching hearts and undimmed eyes; we stand at Armageddon, and we battle for the Lord!" Now you see why convention organizers hid barbed wire in the bunting on the stage. *(Library of Congress)*

Life was good for Huey Long in the summer of 1935. But he was dissatisfied with the quality of the cocktails at the swanky Hotel New Yorker, where he stayed on his many trips to the city to broadcast his populist broadsides on NBC Radio. His solution was perfectly Longian: He had the bartender from the Sazerac Bar in New Orleans, Sam Guarino, flown to New York (at taxpayer expense, of course) to put on a clinic for making the Ramos gin fizz, a sickly-sweet cocktail that includes orange flower water, milk, and powdered sugar. Patrons and the press lapped it up. *(Getty Images: Bettmann/Contributor)*

On the night of August 27, 1935, Senator Huey Long talked one of President Franklin Roosevelt's key initiatives in Congress into the ground. The master of the filibuster, Long had held forth for nearly six hours until his fellow senators gave in and pulled the bill. Long left Washington shortly thereafter to tend to his political kingdom back home in Louisiana. After jamming through a bill of his own in the statehouse on September 8, Long was killed by the son-in-law of a judge Long had ruined for opposing him. *(Library of Congress)*

America met forty-three-year-old governor George Wallace in June of 1963, when he stood in the doorway of the University of Alabama's Foster Auditorium, where he symbolically refused the command of Deputy Attorney General Nicholas Katzenbach, who had come from Washington with an order from President Kennedy desegregating the school. Wallace would stand aside, but only after he had the photo-op and got the chance to make a speech. Wallace in that moment coupled his two most powerful weapons: white racial resentment and contempt for the eastern liberal elite. *(Library of Congress)*

Pat Buchanan is seen here in his natural habitat: surrounded by the media in New Hampshire. Buchanan's blend of populist nationalism and Roman Catholic cultural crusading made him a natural fit with New Hampshire Republicans, who helped him to a strong second-place showing in 1992 against a sitting president in the state's primary and an outright win in 1996. His penchant for lobbing verbal Molotov cocktails at his fellow Republicans made him a natural fit for reporters hungry for fresh copy on the campaign trail. *(Getty Images: John Mottern/Stringer)*

Ross Perot was riding high in July of 1992, leading in the polls despite not having officially declared his candidacy. But then he dropped out of the race, citing some spooky-sounding stuff about doctored photos of his daughter. But his campaign stayed in it, working to get Perot on the ballot in all fifty states. As he prepared to get in for real, he turned to the same place where he launched the non-campaign-campaign in the first place: CNN's *Larry King Live*. Perot found, though, that his summertime episode had cost him much of his initial support. *(Getty Images: Shelly Katz/Contributor)*

CHAPTER FIVE

Enemies Foreign

(And Damned Sure Domestic)

Thousands of men and women were packed into Serb Hall in Southside Milwaukee singing "Dixie" in Polish.

The man they were serenading on the night of April 1, 1964, was Alabama governor George Wallace, who was there campaigning one week ahead of the state's Democratic presidential primary.

Wallace had taken the Confederate flags off of his airplane and replaced the slogan on its side, "Stand up for Alabama," with "Stand up for America." But he needn't have worried. His fans loved him just the way he was.

"Och, chciałbym być w Dixie..."

Wallace had made a belated entry into the contest about a month before when he realized a couple of things on a visit for a speaking engagement in Madison. First, it was shockingly easy to get on the ballot. A candidate just needed sixty voters to sign on the dotted line. Second, Wisconsin, with a black population of just 3 percent, was surprisingly friendly territory for a race-baiting southern populist.

Milwaukee's Southside was an ethnic enclave inside a metropolitan area that was primarily of German and British extraction. These were the Serbs and the Croats and the Poles whose parents had emigrated to boomtown Milwaukee three and four decades earlier. You may have seen the fictionalized version of the neighborhood in the sitcom *Laverne and Shirley*.

The Southside was gritty but intensely proud. And it was also on the front lines of a simmering racial conflict with the city's ascendant black population—a group that had grown fivefold to more than seventy-five thousand souls from 1940 to 1960.

Whether the harms are real or imagined, it is the Americans closest to the bottom of the social ladder who most acutely feel the pangs of social change. And if you think that your position is precarious, that tends to make you an easier target for demagogues. Where there is resentment, there is fear. And where there is fear, there will be anger.

School busing, as would be the case in so many northern cities over the next two decades, was a big part of the alarm in Milwaukee's blue-collar neighborhoods. A 1960 survey by the local school board found that 90 percent of inner-city students were black, and by 1964 educators had moved to integrate classrooms under intense pressure from civil rights groups, including school walkouts and protests. This was met with a furious response in the Southside and elsewhere.

In his campaign visits Wallace embraced the strife, saying that the de facto segregation of Wisconsin was just a less forthright version of the de jure segregation of his native state. "In the South," he told one audience sympathetically but judgmentally, "we believe in segregation and we say so."

But there was more going on here than just racial resentment. By this point, Wallace, a national figure since his June

1963 showdown with President Kennedy over integrating the University of Alabama, had fused his support for segregation with an intense form of anticommunism and a disdain for the federal government that bordered on the paranoiac.

Wallace had said in his inaugural address as governor in January of that year, "In the name of the greatest people that have ever trod this earth, I draw the line in the dust and toss the gauntlet before the feet of tyranny, and I say segregation now, segregation tomorrow, segregation forever."

We remember the bit about "segregation now," but for Wallace and his growing cadre of followers, the part about what they said was the "tyranny" of the federal government was becoming increasingly important.

Whether he believed it or not, Wallace's suggestion was that in his battle with the race mixers of Alabama, he had uncovered a deeper conspiracy with ties running all the way from the White House to the Kremlin. The message struck a chord in Wisconsin.

Remember, this was a state that until just seven years earlier had been represented in the Senate by Joseph McCarthy. "Reds" and "pinkos" were already a well-established part of the Wisconsin political lexicon long before Wallace got to town. And what better place for an anticommunist crusade than among Eastern European immigrants anguishing over their relatives trapped behind the Iron Curtain?

Wallace's rival in the primary was technically Governor John Reynolds. But Reynolds was only a stand-in for President Lyndon Johnson, since in those days it was considered unseemly for a sitting president to contest a primary vote. Only sixteen states held Democratic primaries that year, with most still using the old-fashioned (and undemocratic) convention system.

(While Wallace was exploiting new avenues for direct democracy in his party, he was using old-style machine politics against Johnson back home. He arranged it so that the incoming president's name did not even appear on the Alabama ballot in the general election.)

Wallace had missed the contest in New Hampshire, but saw opportunities on the calendar beyond Wisconsin. Indiana, Maryland, and other states where working-class whites lived in close proximity to substantial African American populations looked promising.

Wallace told aides that if he could get the right kind of launch out of Wisconsin, he could build momentum and eventually draw the president out into open combat and maybe even a contested convention. There, southern delegates could join forces with Wallace's northern supporters and snatch the title.

Johnson did not entirely disagree. He was watching Wisconsin closely and sending instructions to Reynolds to get out and fight.

One of Wallace's biggest boosters in the Badger State was Bronko Gruber, who kept a popular tavern on the Southside and had become a militant Wallace man. It was Gruber who arranged the event at Serb Hall, and it was he who took the stage to the strains of "Dixie" à la Warsaw.

Before Gruber could introduce the candidate, he had some

business to settle with two African American protesters who had come to the event. They remained seated in stony silence as "The Star-Spangled Banner" was sung. According to the *Milwaukee Journal* account, at Gruber's beckoning, the crowd turned on the men with loud booing and hissing, punctuated with a shout of "Send them back to Africa!"

"I live on Walnut Street and three weeks ago one of my friends was assaulted by three of your countrymen or whatever you want to call them," Gruber said. "They beat up old ladies, eighty-three years old, they rape our women folk, how long can we tolerate this?"

Wallace knew he was home.

The governor, stretching himself to his full five feet seven inches, sent the already overheated crowd into new ecstasies of anger, railing against the federal government, atheism, communism, "pointy-headed" East Coast intellectuals, and many of the other tropes that would become hallmarks of this presidential run and the three more that would follow it.

Wallace never mentioned the ugliness with the protesters and did not dwell much on the subject of race. He was crafting a new northern strategy on the fly, and it seemed to be working. According to historian Dan Carter, Wallace saw the future at Serb Hall.

"He had been right all along: these chunky Serbs and Hungarians and Poles, these hardworking Catholics, these *Yankees*," Carter wrote, "had embraced him with the same adoration that marked his passage among the masses of white Alabamians."

The speech made headlines from coast to coast and generated enormous buzz in the state, enough so that both Johnson and Attorney General Robert Kennedy felt obliged to issue a statement of public support for Reynolds in its wake.

It was enough to prevent utter catastrophe for Johnson, but not enough to stop Wallace from getting a shockingly large one-third of the vote on election day. He told supporters that they had "won without winning" and declared, "If I ever had to leave Alabama, I'd want to live on the Southside of Milwaukee!"

And perhaps most surprising in Wallace's strong showing was how much support he drew beyond the Southside. Yes, he did best in blue-collar ethnic neighborhoods, but his performance in wealthier suburbs to the west in Waukesha County was perhaps the best indication of how strong was the sentiment against Johnson and the Democratic establishment.

When similar results came in later that spring in Indiana and Maryland, it became clear to both Johnson and Wallace that the Democratic Party's transition from a party dominated by southern whites and northern union members to one with African American voters at its center was going to be very painful.

The election of 1968 four years later would prove that point lavishly. Wallace used the time between campaigns to shift his focus even further beyond segregation in Alabama. The growing unrest on campuses and city streets and deepening concerns about America's failures in Vietnam would allow him lots of leeway in making his shift from one of the last of the old-time segregationists and into the vanguard of a populist movement with a new set of fears and resentments. He knew he could count on the votes of the actual racists without actively seeking their support, but was now ready to move beyond racism as his animating cause.

Before we move ahead, though, we need to consider what brought Wallace to this moment.

Just as we would be letting ourselves off too easily if we saw Wallace strictly in terms of his bigotry, it would let him off too cheaply not to pause here to consider the scope of his cynical barbarism in context. For that, we need to look at the world Wallace and his southern political contemporaries inherited.

Historians have for decades juxtaposed the virulent racism that Wallace used to advance his career with the relative absence of race-baiting in the career of his populist predecessor, Huey Long.

Long was certainly more racially cool than Wallace and many of Wallace's contemporaries. But when the Kingfish burst on the scene, issues of race tended to matter less because the ugly work of disenfranchising black voters had already been finished for some time and the struggle for civil rights was still two or three decades away.

Vanderbilt University historian Robert Margo estimated that the Louisiana electorate had been about half African American in 1890, but less than a tenth of a percent by 1910.

White residents of New Orleans had rioted in 1900 in response to a shooting spree by a black resident, marking the end of Louisiana's less draconian segregation laws. The "grass eaters," as the members of the Long faction would come to call avowed racists in politics—because they'd rather stand in a field and eat grass than live with blacks as their equals—had already succeeded in purging black voters.

While Long and other southern populists may have opposed their efforts in their time, it is worth remembering that the power of Protestant poor whites from upstate Louisiana, North Alabama, or the Georgia hills would have been far less in an integrated electorate. With black voters shut out, Long's "boys at the forks of the creek" had their way.

The arc on racial politics in the South goes something like this:

Freedmen were thrust into relative political equality at the point of Army bayonets during Reconstruction from 1865 to 1873 (earlier for some areas, later for others).

A period of brutal but relatively disorganized retaliation by whites followed the departure of military occupiers. This was the rise of the real Ku Klux Klan—the one of lynching and vigilantism, not the tiki torch poseurs of our time. Fueled by deep resentment toward their military occupiers and the carpetbaggers and black Republicans they empowered, former Confederates meted out painful retribution.

But in places where black southerners had amassed significant numbers and sufficient resources, they were able to persist with some privileges of citizenship. North Carolina, Virginia, Texas, and Louisiana all had robust African American enfranchisement relative to their fellow former Confederate states.

The turn of the century, though, brought a new kind of

systemic oppression. It was rooted in pseudoscientific ratio-nalizations of white racial supremacy and, ironically, in the improving economic fortunes of the South.

As the region industrialized during and after the boom-and-bust 1890s, it produced new centers of power and leaders deeply enmeshed with the Democratic Party and with them the suppression of black human rights. This was when Jim Crow came of age and town squares and avenues were newly adorned with statues of Confederate heroes from fifty years before.

This American apartheid may not have been constitutional, but it was legal. It carried the force of governments from the tiniest hamlets to the largest cities. Birmingham, Alabama, had gone from a population of less than 40,000 in 1900 to nearly 180,000 in 1920 with a marriage of modernity in industry with medievalism on race. A status quo of oppres-sion was forged across the region, one that would survive rapid technological and cultural changes in the wider world and two world wars.

But by the end of the Second World War, the era of quiet seething was coming to an end. Black Americans who had gone north for work or joined the military to fight fascistic racism abroad came home less willing to maintain an old truce predicated on their own submission to tyranny.

The Nazis had absolutely ruined what had been conven-tional American thinking (both North and South) on racial superiority and eugenics. Threats to the system were mount-ing internally from a new generation of African American lawyers and activists who were starting to split the seams of institutionalized racism, but also externally from an activist federal government.

You could pick any number of signal moments for the change in southern politics, but I like July 26, 1948. That's when President Harry Truman issued Executive Order 9981 and began the desegregation of the U.S. military. The remaining old-school, hard-line racists like Senator Theodore Bilbo of Mississippi had set this as an inviolable line. Bilbo was primarily concerned with the "mongrelization" of Anglo-Saxon Americans.

"The South stands for blood, for the preservation of the blood of the white race," Bilbo, a holdover from the turn of the century's enthusiastic bigots, wrote in his 1946 screed *Take Your Choice: Separation or Mongrelization*. "To preserve her blood, the white South must absolutely deny social equality to the Negro regardless of what his individual accomplishments might be. This is the premise—openly and frankly stated—upon which Southern policy is based."

So sayeth the chairman of the Senate Committee on Pensions...

To Bilbo and his younger disciples (including future senator Robert Byrd of West Virginia, who would later lament his enthusiastic support for a demagogue so vile), letting black and white troops serve together would be one step closer to the end of miscegenation laws that kept blacks and whites from marrying in sixteen states for another decade. When Truman acted, it unleashed a torrent of the same kind of lurid, fake social science. But the racists were right about one thing: It was the beginning of the end for their way of life.

Within six years, school segregation would be forbidden. Within eight years, segregation of public transportation would be declared unconstitutional. Within twelve years, segregation of places of public accommodation was disallowed. Within sixteen years, the Civil Rights Act would be the law of the land.

After decades of status quo in which populists like Long could tiptoe around questions of race and institutional segregation while still benefiting from its effects at the ballot box, the 1950s would mark a return of the grass eaters.

When Huey's brother Earl lost his 1959 race for a fourth term as governor to a candidate in league with the racist kooks, it marked the end of the line of compromise on matters of race in the Democratic Party. The longer-term future would belong to absolutists for equality. But in the near term, it was the age of the absolutists for segregation, fire-breathers like Wallace.

What's funny about Wallace, though, is that he did not start out with flames on his tongue.

As a delegate to the 1948 Democratic convention, Wallace did not participate in the walkout by other southerners to protest Truman's military integration. Wallace did support South Carolina governor Strom Thurmond that fall as a Dixiecrat (as the States' Rights Democratic Party was better known). But that was to be expected. Truman wasn't even on the ballot in Alabama. It was all part of the larger protest that southern

Democrats assumed would throw the election to Republican nominee Thomas Dewey and teach Democrats a lesson about respecting their southern base. Of course, Dewey did not defeat Truman and Democrats learned an entirely different lesson about white southerners: They were expendable.

But that was all still off in the future for a young, ambitious Wallace.

As a judge in the early 1950s, he was known for his decorous treatment of African American lawyers and relatively merciful sentences for some black defendants. He even secured an appointment to the board of trustees for the all-black Tuskegee Institute.

When he first ran for governor in 1958, it was not on a platform of segregation, but rather one of economic populism little different from that of Long or William Jennings Bryan. Wallace's stinging defeat—aided by accusations that he was insufficiently racist as a judge and soft on Truman—changed him. He was reborn as a race hustler.

"You know, I tried to talk about good roads and good schools and all these things that have been part of my career, and nobody listened," Wallace told a supporter about his change of heart. "And then I began talking about n———s, and they stomped the floor."

Here we meet the central problem we face with populism: What do we do when what's popular is wrong? What the people—or at least the enfranchised white people—of Alabama wanted was wicked. Wallace knew it. He knew it so well that he would despair of his views later and recant. But the only way for him to climb the ladder of power was to give the people what they wanted.

John Adams knew about such things, and had gone to great pains to warn the populists of his day about the George Wallaces to come. In an 1814 letter to Virginia Anti-Federalist John Taylor, one of the most influential agrarian populists of the early republic, the former president was unsparing.

"It is in vain to say that democracy is less vain, less proud, less selfish, less ambitious, or less avaricious than aristocracy or monarchy," Adams wrote. "It is not true, in fact, and nowhere appears in history. Those passions are the same in all men, under all forms of simple government, and when unchecked, produce the same effects of fraud, violence, and cruelty."

And let me tell you, if you wanted to see fraud, violence, and cruelty, the politics of Alabama in the days of Wallace would surely fit the bill.

America met forty-three-year-old Wallace standing in the doorway of the University of Alabama's Foster Auditorium, where he symbolically refused the command of Deputy Attorney General Nicholas Katzenbach, who had come from Washington with an order from President Kennedy desegregating the school.

What Wallace found, though, was that a lot of Americans who weren't as deeply invested in the issue of legal segregation still resented people like Katzenbach, a product of Princeton, Yale, and Oxford, not to mention powerful family connections. These were the eastern elites who, as Wallace would say so often, "look down their noses" at ordinary Americans.

Johnson was able to box out Wallace in 1964 with relatively little difficulty, but Wallace would be back and better able to exploit the grievances and sense of persecution in a growing sector of the electorate. He had picked up race-baiting at the beginning of the decade to get ahead in Alabama; now he was ready to shift his focus again to make his play in the rest of the country.

What was selling with a big segment of the rest of America just then was resentment toward the Nicholas Katzenbachs of the world.

Prevented by term limits from seeking another term as governor in 1966, Wallace had gotten his wife, Lurleen, elected in his place. Knowing that his home fires were burning strong, the first gentleman of Alabama was free to start crisscrossing the country in service of his 1968 presidential campaign.

The influx of black voters to the Democratic Party in the wake of civil rights legislation made it even less likely that Wallace could capture his party's nomination. To circumvent that problem and to accommodate his new friends on the far right, Wallace opted to run a third-party bid and founded the American Independent Party.

Despite Wallace's surprising popularity with blue-collar northern voters, his strategy was not very different from that of Thurmond's Dixiecrat run in 1948. Wallace knew he was unlikely to win the presidency outright, but believed that if he were to win enough support in the South, he could force a deadlock in the Electoral College and throw the race to the House of Representatives.

There, he could use his leverage to extract concessions on segregation and other considerations in exchange for his support. He envisioned a scenario in which he would be able to get Johnson "over a barrel."

But then things changed.

Enfeebled by the growing opposition to the war in Vietnam, Johnson showed poorly in the 1968 New Hampshire primary against antiwar candidate Senator Eugene McCarthy. Johnson's fizzle prompted Robert Kennedy to drop his support for Johnson and declare his own candidacy in March of that year. That, in turn, prompted Johnson to drop out of the contest in favor of his vice president and the lead author of the Civil Rights Act, Hubert Humphrey.

This was all good news for Wallace, who then knew that the Democrats would be nominating a northern liberal, whether it was Humphrey, Kennedy, or McCarthy.

Republicans, scalded by their 1964 nomination of conservative senator Barry Goldwater, had a taste for moderation. Richard Nixon, former vice president and narrow loser of the 1960 campaign, was considered the safe course for the GOP between the liberal New York governor Nelson Rockefeller and Goldwater heir California governor Ronald Reagan.

Kennedy was assassinated on the night he won the California primary in June, just two months after the murder of Martin Luther King Jr. Kennedy's death all but assured Humphrey of the nomination.

Wallace could have hardly asked for a better scenario. The Democrats had nominated a mild-mannered liberal from

Minnesota at a Chicago convention marred by antiwar protests and the brutal police suppression of the demonstrations. The Republicans were lined up behind an uninspiring retread. At a time when antiestablishment sentiment was running high, the major parties had picked establishmentarians of the first order.

Wallace was understaffed and underfunded by comparison to his major-party opponents, but he was not without some advantages.

Americans today bemoan the way that social media facilitates the spread of false information and conspiracy theories. Things were better, we are told, when a handful of trusted sources vetted and disseminated the news. And in some ways that's true, since the profusion of news sources has allowed Americans to retreat into partisan cocoons where they can go unmolested by opposing points of view.

But don't ever kid yourself that ours is the first era of fake news.

In 1958, retired candy maker Robert Welch started the John Birch Society, named for an Army intelligence officer killed by communist forces in China just after the end of World War II. Welch called Birch the first casualty of the Cold War.

Welch recruited eleven other wealthy businessmen to form the society, which focused not so much on developing a large rank-and-file membership as on cultivating a relatively small number of dedicated true believers.

Even so, at its peak the John Birch Society would boast at

least one hundred thousand members in chapters across the country. New recruits were given a book of Welch's teachings and shown films outlining his worldview.

"Both the U.S. and Soviet governments are controlled by the same furtive conspiratorial cabal of internationalists, greedy bankers, and corrupt politicians," Welch wrote in *The Blue Book of the John Birch Society*. "If left unexposed, the traitors inside the U.S. government would betray the country's sovereignty to the United Nations for a collectivist New World Order, managed by a 'one-world socialist government.'"

If any of that sounds familiar to you today, it's because the Birchers proved remarkably successful at pushing these concepts into the mainstream. They were hardly the first to warn of the dangers of internationalism, but they were enormously efficient at condensing and distributing the point of view.

Here's how the *New York Times* described the reach of the society in the mid-1960s: "a budget of $8 million a year and 270 paid employees, many of them working out of a headquarters in Belmont, Mass.; a book publishing house; two monthly publications; a speakers' bureau; a radio program and 400 Birch-owned bookstores."

You couldn't exactly say that the society was part of Wallace's campaign organization, but it was close. The message of the Wallace campaign was increasingly close to that of the Birchers, and campaign staffers and volunteers often came straight out of Birch chapters.

Wallace kept "Stand up for America" as his slogan in 1968, but augmented it with a new rallying cry: "Send 'em a message!" Yes, it acknowledged the long-shot nature of the campaign, but it also brilliantly tapped into the idea that with just one vote, supporters could put the "pointy-headed bureaucrats who can't park a bicycle straight" on notice.

Having declared that there wasn't "a dime's worth of difference" between the two major parties, Wallace threw open the doors to his new party for anyone who felt that the game had been rigged against them—as historian Michael Kazin put it, the voters who "felt their good jobs, their modest homes, and their personal safety were under siege both from liberal authorities above and angry minorities below."

Or, as Wallace's American Independent Party platform would put it, "The average American [is] confused and dismayed when these leaders desert the principle of government for the people and dedicate themselves to minority appeasement as the country burns and decays."

There was pretty strong evidence of burn and decay in 1968, too. Riots swept through dozens of cities in the wake of King's assassination, campus protests were a constant presence, and the Black Panthers were grabbing headlines. The news from Vietnam was also bad with the Tet offensive and more than sixteen thousand American servicemen killed over the course of the year.

To Wallace and his supporters, the communists were winning the Cold War overseas, in the streets, and in the halls of power in Washington.

His campaign advisers would urge Wallace to focus his efforts on winning across the South, emphasizing Florida,

Tennessee, North Carolina, and Virginia as potential pick-ups beyond his presumptive base in Alabama, Mississippi, Georgia, South Carolina, Louisiana, and Arkansas. If Wallace won most of the electoral votes of the former Confederacy, he would be poised to play kingmaker in what was expected to be a close race between Humphrey and Nixon.

Wallace, though, was thinking bigger. He remembered what he saw in Wisconsin four years prior and was also reveling in the extraordinary press coverage he was getting in his travels across the country. Quotes that reporters repeated to viewers and readers for shock value did not offend his target voters, but instead excited them.

He called long-haired hippie protesters "sweetie," promised to run over any "anarchists" whose protests impeded his motorcade, and said that the only four-letter words they didn't know were "w-o-r-k" and "s-o-a-p." Audiences and voters at home ate it up.

Wallace was showing considerable strength in the polls, passing the 20 percent threshold late in the summer and approaching a quarter of the vote. Union members were increasingly unwilling to back Humphrey, and right-wing Republicans were starting to warm up to Wallace. It was the kind of left-right fusion campaign that many have attempted but none have come so close to pulling off.

Then two important things happened. First, Nixon and Humphrey started to take Wallace very seriously. Nixon shifted his rhetoric and strategy to position himself as the candidate of "law and order." Humphrey began an intense outreach to union members. Second, Wallace let his inner Bircher get the better of him with his vice presidential selection.

Wallace's campaign aides had been looking for a running mate who would either intensify southern support or make inroads in border states. Atop the list was former Kentucky governor Happy Chandler. A onetime segregationist, Chandler had changed his views. He had even overseen the integration of Major League Baseball as the game's commissioner after World War II. He was what Wallace was not: moderate, averse to controversy, and respected across multiple demographic strata.

One campaign aide put the argument for Chandler to Wallace this way, according to Carter's history: "We have all the nuts in the country.... We could get some decent people—you working one side of the street and he working the other side."

They eventually convinced Wallace to accept the moderate Chandler as his running mate. But when the news leaked ahead of the convention, Wallace's new right-wing supporters were immediately outraged. Chandler without segregation was just a typical liberal Democrat in their eyes.

Wallace swiftly withdrew the offer (though Chandler would claim he had never formally agreed to join Wallace in the first place) and set about persuading his real first choice, retired Air Force general Curtis LeMay.

"Bombs Away" LeMay had been Wallace's commanding officer during the Second World War. Their mission was to break the will of the Japanese populace and government with massive bombardments from squadrons of B-29 Superfortresses.

After the war, LeMay had emerged as a prominent Cold War hawk. He had led the Strategic Air Command and held other high-level posts in the Pentagon, repeatedly clashing with the Kennedy and Johnson administrations about the use of force against communists in Cuba and Vietnam. He favored massive bombardment of the kind he had used in Japan, but found no political appetite for such moves.

When LeMay was pushed out of the Air Force in 1965 he was seen as a martyr for the anticommunist cause and became a favorite of the Birchers and other anti-red hard-liners. It looked like a perfect fit for Wallace.

LeMay instead proved to be an unmitigated disaster. He had written in his 1965 autobiography that if the North Vietnamese did not cease their attacks, the United States should "bomb them back into the Stone Age." He reinforced this idea on the campaign trail, saying in his first interview as Wallace's running mate that Americans had too many "phobias" about the use of nuclear weapons. Later, he would suggest that using nukes in Vietnam might be necessary.

Wallace's support dropped like the payload out of the belly of a B-29. Nixon and Humphrey were both promising to bring the nightmarish slog of the war to the end, and here was the populist party promising to escalate it.

As the fall wore on, it was now obvious that Wallace wasn't going to make it a three-way race. But rather than retreat and run a Dixiecrat-style effort in the South, he was determined to remain a national candidate, campaigning in places he had no chance of winning.

Was he already thinking about 1972? Probably. Was he addicted to the attention? Most definitely. Did he reciprocate the love his most ardent supporters felt for him? Absolutely.

Wallace would run for president twice more as a Democrat. His 1972 bid was cut short by the bullet of a would-be assassin that severed his spinal cord. He would seek the presidency again in 1976, launching his last crusade in, appropriately enough, Milwaukee's Serb Hall with old Bronko Gruber by his side. Wallace was by then in a wheelchair and Gruber wizened by age.

But those were mostly symbolic campaigns, efforts to recapture the chaotic energy of 1968—the moment when a real revolution seemed possible, the time when some of the voters whom Nixon would come to call the "silent majority" didn't feel the need to be so silent.

The week before the election Wallace took his show to New York's Madison Square Garden and got exactly the kind of spectacle he must have dreamed of. The place was packed to the rafters with more than twenty thousand supporters. Protesters thronged the building. Some three thousand police officers had to ring the venue just to keep the peace.

Wallace gave them the old-time religion—a punched-up version of the same speech he gave in Milwaukee four years before. He thundered against the elites and "left-wing intellectuals and communist professors who advocate a victory for the Vietcong." He denounced, as always, the news media that were encouraging "the rebellion in our streets." He promised to use the power of the people to crush the "anarchists who are stealing the American way of life."

The *New York Times* talked to several attendees who had come for the show, including Richard Brady, a police officer who traveled down from Poughkeepsie: "'I was in the Navy for six and a half years,' said Mr. Brady, his face growing dark with rage. 'You sing "God Bless America" and say the Pledge of Allegiance and you really believe it—and some people think you're a kook. That's why I'm here tonight.'"

Brady and most of the other attendees must have known that Wallace wasn't going to win New York—he would get just 5 percent of the vote in the Empire State—but that didn't keep them from attending. They were there for the same heady rush that brought Wallace there, too: to stand up and yawp right in the face of the cosmopolitan elites.

Wallace would end up as one of the most successful third-party candidates in history, drawing almost 14 percent of the popular vote and carrying five states: Arkansas, Louisiana, Mississippi, Georgia, and Alabama. But Nixon carried the rest of the South and enough electoral votes for a decisive victory over Humphrey.

What Wallace had really succeeded in doing, though, was showing the potential power of all of the Richard Bradys out there—traditionalist members of the middle class who felt excluded and victimized by a liberal dominant culture.

American populism had mostly been the province of the left, focusing as it did on economic inequality. But Wallace had midwifed a new American movement of right-wing populism, the very same one we still see today. The center of gravity for American populism wasn't going to be about fighting against economic power but rather cultural change.

"Send 'em a message," Wallace said. It's doubtful whether the elites of Manhattan or Hollywood really heard what he was saying. But Republicans, starting with Nixon and his speechwriter Buchanan, definitely got it.

CHAPTER SIX

The Avengers

(Not So Happy Warriors)

By the second day of May 1992, there were fourteen thousand federal troops deployed in the city of Los Angeles.

Marine riflemen and light armor units from Camp Pendleton to the south and Army infantrymen and cavalrymen from Fort Ord to the north convened in the city and joined forces with thousands of National Guard troops who had already been fighting rioters for two days.

President George H. W. Bush had addressed the nation on the night before, making plain the troops' purpose: "I will use whatever force is necessary to restore order. What is going on in L.A. must and will stop. As your president, I guarantee you this violence will end."

It did end, but only after astonishing carnage.

It had been more than twenty years since Americans had watched scenes like those beaming out of Southern California. Wanton looting. Random killing. Armored units rolling down city streets.

By Sunday, at least four dozen people had been killed, more than two thousand were injured, and an estimated twelve thousand had been arrested. Authorities reported that 3,767 structures had burned in the fires set that week—the world's first $1 billion riot.

But unlike with the violence that had racked so many

cities in the 1960s, Americans could watch the firestorm in L.A. around the clock. They could see it with terrible intimacy, thanks to new highly portable video equipment, but they could also watch from the disquieting remove of news helicopters circling above.

The riots began because of what a private citizen had recorded on his own video camera the year before when four white Los Angeles police officers brutally beat a black man who had fled from a traffic stop. When the anarchy that followed those officers' acquittals was over, the lasting memory was of the footage of a white man who had unknowingly driven his tractor-trailer into the flashpoint of the riot. Rioters dragged him from the cab of his rig and beat him nearly to death as looters, giddy with their hauls, scurried past.

Just eight years after Southern California had delivered Ronald Reagan's "Morning in America" and the euphoric success of the Los Angeles Olympics, the city horrified the nation with a vision of a failed society.

And if you're looking for a presidential candidate to match a failed society vibe, Pat Buchanan's your man.

Buchanan had joined the 1992 presidential campaign in December of the previous year in what seemed like something between a stunt and a protest. Bush had betrayed conservatives with a 1990 budget deal that broke the pledge he made to secure their support in the 1988 presidential election. They were ready for revenge. Speechwriter Peggy Noonan had been too good at crafting a memorable line—"Read my lips: No new taxes"—for Bush's convention speech. When the president reneged, Noonan's punchy line boomeranged and knocked the incumbent right out of his topsiders.

Buchanan was in a good position to help in the pummeling. He may or may not have been the most influential conservative pundit in the country at the time, but he was certainly the most visible.

He did battle every weeknight on CNN's *Crossfire* with his liberal counterpart, Michael Kinsley. Saturdays saw him scrapping on the network's *Capital Gang*, while Sundays were for roughhousing on *The McLaughlin Group* on PBS. Buchanan wrote a column syndicated in hundreds of newspapers across the country, churned out weekly newsletters, and for years had done daily commentaries for NBC radio. If he wasn't America's most famous man of the right, it wasn't for lack of trying.

But his candidacy was no mere publicity stunt, nor was it just some kind of taxpayer protest over Bush's loose lips.

Buchanan was a journalist by training and disposition, but he had already changed American politics before he became a talking head. As an adviser and speechwriter to Richard Nixon, he was instrumental in crafting the successful outreach to potential George Wallace voters in 1968. He was also a key player in developing the "silent majority" culture war strategy for 1972 that helped Nixon to the biggest landslide victory since FDR's first reelection.

This strategy is too easily dismissed as only an appeal to the racial animus that was still simmering among some southerners. Buchanan and Nixon knew that they could count on the support of the remaining segregationists who had rejected their old home in the Democratic Party with the same vehemence that black voters had embraced it.

Wallace had made his bones as a bigot, which held him back with better-educated voters. But he saw the huge potential of exploiting the class resentments and cultural anxieties of blue-collar white voters in the North. In the late 1960s they were increasingly willing to see themselves as victims of both elites and the cultural upheaval all around them. Nixon, a moderate who had been Ike's sidekick for eight years, had none of Wallace's baggage. He could have the country club and the beer hall at the same time.

Buchanan wouldn't have the same advantages as his old boss.

As an author, Buchanan has publicly praised Adolf Hitler's gifts of leadership and sense of history. He cast considerable blame for the Second World War and the Holocaust on the globalists of the day, Winston Churchill and Franklin Roosevelt. "Hitler wanted to end the war in 1940," Buchanan would later write, "almost two years before the trains began to roll to the camps."

He had also been an unabashed ethnic nationalist in his writings. "Who speaks for the Euro-Americans who founded the United States?" he asked in a June 1990 column. "Is it not time to take America back?"

Buchanan defended Klansman turned gubernatorial candidate David Duke for holding the same outré positions on foreign aid, welfare, affirmative action, and immigration that Buchanan did. "The national press calls these positions 'code words' for racism," he wrote in a column, "but in the hard times in Louisiana, Duke's message comes across as middle class, meritocratic, populist and nationalist."

This was the intellectual high-wire act that made Buchanan a star of the political talk show circuit. Yes, he was a brawler. But his real gift was as a provocateur. Buchanan knew how to draw out the accusations and then turn them right back around on the accuser.

He *of course* wouldn't really defend Duke, who was an open bigot. And *of course* he detested Hitler and anti-Semitism—and why are you trying to shut down debate by just accusing people of racism? And are you suggesting his hardworking, decent voters are racists for supporting him? We're just talking about immigration policy here, people. You can't just go around calling people *deplorable*, after all.

And if the actual racists end up hearing the dog whistle he swears he's not blowing, well…their votes count, too.

Buchanan knows well that there's little that right-wingers love more than to hear candidates batter the press. And by his reasoning, the accusations of bigotry against him were proof that he was winning the fight. For right-wing populists, then and now, the "mainstream media" is often the best enemy to have. Being at war with the media discredits even legitimate criticism in the eyes of supporters and allows the candidates and their supporters to share not just the warming crackle of resentment but also a sense of victimhood.

And it's not a new idea. One of Buchanan's memos drafted in the wake of Nixon's 1972 blowout victory called for using the power of the federal government to clamp down on the television networks for "a strategy against their monopoly control, and a thought-out program for cleaning out public television of that clique of Nixon-haters who have managed to nest there at public expense."

(In the same memo, Buchanan called for asserting political control over the IRS and purging the federal bureaucracy of the anti-Nixon resistance, so let's just say he was thinking big back in the day.)

At a still-famous rally just before the New Hampshire primary in 1996, Buchanan didn't open on taxes or trade or his opponent's weaknesses or globalism. He wanted to know if folks had seen him on TV. "Did you see the Brinkley show today?" Buchanan asked the over-capacity crowd jammed into a Nashua, New Hampshire, conference room, referring to ABC's Sunday staple *This Week with David Brinkley.*

To a casual viewer, the show would have seemed like a rough workout session for Buchanan that morning, with the panel coming after him hard on the usual stuff: the support for his campaign by white supremacists ("I can't control who supports me"); his avowed creationism ("You may believe you're descended from monkeys, but I don't believe it"); and his hard line against gay rights ("Love the sinner, hate the sin").

Oof.

But when he got onstage, Buchanan was absolutely jazzed about the show.

"George Will started yapping at me like a little poodle," he said, repeating the poodle line a couple of times to make sure the boisterous crowd got it. "And I had to take the newspaper and roll it up and hit him with it once or twice." The audience roared its approval.

The *Washington Post*'s Joel Achenbach was there to describe the scene: "The room was too small to contain the event. Rage became condensed. Buchanan looked as if he might squirt through the ceiling."

No trait has likely served Buchanan better in his political career than the skill he honed for decades as a media cage fighter. But when he hit the stage at New Hampshire's capital, Concord, on December 10, 1991, to launch his first presidential run, he did not project the gleefully combative political talk show panelist whom Americans saw every day. Instead, he presented himself as a far-right intellectual revolutionary who had been in close-quarters combat with the Republican establishment for a generation.

And he wasn't just there to talk about taxes and George Bush's lips, either.

Bush's broken tax pledge didn't rankle Buchanan nearly as much as the president's war with Iraq. The hugely popular war, which lasted just six weeks in January and February 1991, had been a smashing success militarily and politically. It was still the best thing Bush had going for him, especially as the economic slowdown that had begun in the summer of 1990 started gripping voters' wallets more tightly.

In seeking congressional support for the war, Bush had spoken of how it could help forge a "new world order" in the wake of the impending collapse of the Soviet Union. The Iraq conflict, fought with American leadership but under the auspices of the United Nations, could help bring about the kind of global cooperation and control that had eluded leaders since before Woodrow Wilson's failed League of Nations.

Buchanan framed his candidacy around an idea with roots almost as old as Bush's quest for "a world where the rule of law supplants the rule of the jungle." Buchanan's cry that day was "America first," the same words that had once ricocheted from the rafters of rallies against entering the Second World War.

For Buchanan and his fellows, a "new world order" would make America a vassal state to global elites. And for those on the further fringes, it was the stuff of black helicopters, secret government detention camps, and nothing less than the end of America. (As I've said before, don't ever let yourself think that our age is the dawn of fake news and kookism. It just used to come by mail on mimeograph sheets.)

It sounds strange today given the UN's fairly miserable condition and profound weakness, but this was a red-hot issue on the American right twenty-five years ago.

"By the grace of God, America won the Cold War," Buchanan said in his announcement. "But my friends, victory has not brought with it an end to history. Beyond these shores a new world is being born for which our government is unprepared."

Buchanan (quite rightly, as it would turn out) said that the new force that would shape the world after the era of the struggling superpowers was not international cooperation of the kind that defeated fascism and Soviet communism, but rather nationalism. And he said it was time for America to get in on the game: "We must not trade in our sovereignty for a cushioned seat at the head table of anybody's new world order."

One of his favorite causes on the trail was the case of Michael New, an Army medic who refused to wear a United Nations insignia on his uniform and accept foreign command when his unit was deployed from Germany to take part in the UN peacekeeping force assigned to prevent the war in Kosovo from spilling over the border.

New was court-martialed, stripped of his rank, and dishonorably discharged for his disobedience. Buchanan said it was a "travesty" and evidence that the new world order had real designs on American sovereignty.

"I want to say today to all the globalists up there in Tokyo and New York and Paris," Buchanan would say, "when I raise my hand to take that oath of office, your new world order comes crashing down."

Buchanan said that this new order was not just making America the world's policeman, but stripping the dignity, work, and cultural values from blue-collar voters. Free trade, foreign aid, mass immigration, and Wall Street profiteering were breaking America's blue-collar backbone.

New Hampshire was a natural pick for the starting place of Buchanan's crusade to keep Bush from the nomination. It had a large population of working-class white voters, lots of older residents who still remembered the turmoil of the 1960s and 1970s, and was (and still is) one of the most heavily Roman Catholic states, a particularly good fit for the Jesuitical Buchanan.

The state also has a long history of rejecting establishment candidates, even sitting presidents. It was there that Lyndon Johnson's quest for a second full term came to an end. Best of all for Buchanan, New Hampshire is small enough to let an underfunded upstart get attention without a huge television budget or a large professional organization.

Even so, Buchanan surprised everyone, himself included, with his Granite State performance after just two months in the campaign. His nearly 40 percent of the vote was a humbling blow for Bush as an incumbent and filled the members of the insurgency with optimism.

Those hopes would be quickly dashed as the campaign moved south to Georgia and then on to other large states. Buchanan would never again hold Bush under 60 percent in any primary. After getting creamed on Super Tuesday, he wasn't able to pose as a serious contender for the nomination anymore. Moral victories don't pay for campaign ads.

He slogged on through the rest of the primary calendar, though. And by the time it was all done, Buchanan would rack up a quarter of the popular vote, almost three million votes. That was good enough for a handful of delegates and a prime speaking spot on the first night of the Republican National Convention in August. The campaign had been bitter, but Buchanan had promised not to bolt the party or create any disruption, and he was duly rewarded.

Party leaders were also willing to take a chance on giving the pugilistic Buchanan such a high-profile posting because they thought he might have held the key to unlocking millions

of votes sitting on the sidelines. By then, billionaire independent Ross Perot had been out of the race for more than a
month, but Bush had reaped none of the electoral benefit of
his absence. Democratic nominee Bill Clinton had gotten a
substantial boost from Perot's meltdown, but there was bupkis
for Bush.

The conventional wisdom of the day held (probably correctly) that many of those who were *ahem* waiting for Perot
were Buchanan primary voters who couldn't bring themselves
to vote for Bush.

Perot and Buchanan were miles apart on social issues (Perot
was a pro-choicer who favored government funding for poor
women's abortions, gun control, and gay rights) and foreign
policy (Perot favored robust foreign aid and slashing defense
spending even further), but they were strongly agreed in their
opposition to trade and the need for the federal government to
take the reins on economic planning in order to engineer more
manufacturing jobs.

Maybe, Republicans thought, if they let Buchanan blow
off steam about the North American Free Trade Agreement
and the economic woes of working-class voters, it might be a
sign to the Perotists that the GOP was friendlier territory than
they thought.

Suffice it to say that Buchanan went a different way that
night in Houston.

What he had in mind wasn't trade wars, but rather the real
war that had raged in the streets of Los Angeles four months
earlier. Buchanan had visited L.A. in the aftermath of the riots

while campaigning for the state's June primary. Anxiety over the riots—as well as concerns about immigration—would help law-and-order Buchanan to his best finish in a race since March and add some padding to his impressive popular vote total.

In his Houston speech, Buchanan did his duty and endorsed Bush. He also lavished praise on Bush's predecessor, Reagan, whom Buchanan had served for a time as White House communications director. But his real topic was "a cultural war, as critical to the kind of nation we will one day be as was the Cold War itself." And what he had seen in Los Angeles convinced him that the conflict would be painful, but that it could be won.

Buchanan told the crowd and many millions at home—this was in the days when the broadcast networks still carried blowout prime-time convention coverage—the story of visiting the troops of the 18th Cavalry, and meeting two soldiers who "could not have been twenty years old" and hearing their story:

> They had come into Los Angeles late in the evening of the second day, and the rioting was still going on, and two of them walked up a dark street, where the mob had burned and looted every single building on the block but one, a convalescent home for the aged. And the mob was headed in, to ransack and loot the apartments of the terrified old men and women inside.

The troopers came up the street, M-16s at the ready, and the mob threatened and cursed, but the mob retreated, because it had met the one thing that could stop it: force, rooted in justice, and backed by moral courage.

Only a modest cheer went up, but Buchanan pressed on to his finale:

Here were nineteen-year-old boys ready to lay down their lives to stop a mob from molesting old people they did not even know. And as those boys took back the streets of Los Angeles, block by block, my friends, we must take back our cities, and take back our culture, and take back our country.

"Pitchfork Pat" and his followers, whom his campaign had already dubbed the "Buchanan Brigades," would be the equivalent of those troops, fighting block by block through American political and cultural life.

Their foes were not well-intentioned but misguided liberals, but vandals and looters there to steal and destroy America. And you would never, ever compromise with an angry mob. You would only use "force, rooted in justice, backed by moral courage."

The riots had been evidence to Buchanan and millions of Americans that the country was coming undone. It was not a story about one troubled community, but a harrowing vision of the future.

Buchanan wanted to divide into squads and back Democrats down with figurative M-16s. Bush's own speech would be combative by his own standards, even if it was a tangle of procedural mumbo-jumbo. But it was largely focused on his lament that Democrats refused to compromise with him.

Bush wanted to make a deal because, as he said, "Americans are tired of the blame game, tired of people in Washington acting like they're candidates for the next episode of *American Gladiators*." *Groan.* Buchanan, meanwhile, wanted to feed the liberals to the lions.

At the same convention in what would be his final public speech, Reagan tried to summon a more hopeful future, or at least nostalgia for a more optimistic past. "Whatever else history may say about me when I'm gone," he told a teary-eyed crowd, "I hope it will record that I appealed to your best hopes, not your worst fears, to your confidence rather than your doubts."

The Gipper was right about how history would record his legacy, but he and Bush were wrong about the direction their party and the country's politics would take. Buchanan may have never gotten to be the commanding general, but he was right that the war was coming.

Buchanan would lead his little brigade back on the field twice more: a better-organized but equally doomed bid to keep Senate minority leader Bob Dole from winning the Republican nomination in 1996, and as the nominee of

Perot's Reform Party in 2000. The results would never match the promise of 1992.

Donald Trump made his first run for the presidency in 2000, he said, in part to stop Buchanan from taking over Perot's party with the "really staunch right wacko vote," calling Buchanan "a Hitler lover" and "an anti-Semite."

"He doesn't like the blacks, he doesn't like the gays," Trump said dismissively in an exclusive with NBC News in October 1999 announcing his short-lived presidential run. "It's just incredible that anybody could embrace this guy."

It was indeed incredible that Trump would one day embrace the message and methods even if he never embraced the man he had so maligned. Trump, like most in American public life at the turn of the century, assumed that the political future would look more and more like what we saw in the 2000 election: a narrowly divided electorate with sometimes indistinguishable candidates fighting over slivers of persuadable voters.

The Cold War was won, history was done, and all that statecraft would require was deciding how best to manage the bounty of a protracted Pax Americana. But the conventional wisdom was quite wrong and Pitchfork Pat was quite right. In the absence of the structure of a bipolar world, nationalism and smaller, more intense allegiances on the order of the clan and the tribe would fill the space.

Here's how Buchanan's old sparring partner George Will put it back in Buchanan's heyday: "Here is a paradox of contemporary politics. The more successful a society becomes, the more bored it becomes, and the more susceptible it becomes to the stimulus of politicians' claiming that it is really becoming less successful."

Will may have underappreciated the ways in which human beings yearn for visceral connection and purpose more than they even do for comfort and ease, but he certainly is right about the way in which this tribal-style populism thrives in a vacuum. The 9/11 attacks did unite the nation and did imbue us with purpose—but not for long. In place of that short-lived unity and sincerity would arise the culture that had been simmering in the background: a politics that treats members of the opposing party as enemies and disagreements between members of the same party as heresies.

And how do we excuse such ugly treatment toward our fellow Americans? By convincing ourselves that we are in a fight for survival against each other. Grab your M-16 and start applying force and moral courage.

Anyone who was there for Trump's own 2016 convention speech could hear Buchanan loud and clear.

"Our convention occurs at a moment of crisis for our nation," Trump warned. "The attacks on our police, and the terrorism in our cities, threaten our very way of life. Any politician who does not grasp this danger is not fit to lead our country."

There was no smoldering city of Los Angeles to prove Trump's point as there had been for Buchanan twenty-four years earlier, but Trump's brigades were every bit as ready for war as Buchanan's had been.

"I alone can fix it," Trump declared. And the crowd went wild.

CHAPTER SEVEN

Everybody Is Saying

(That Giant Sucking Sound)

Corporate America teems with men and women who don't just have the right answers, they have the *correct* answer.

Anyone who has survived working at a consultancy (or through a contract with one) will know just the folks I mean. You can picture them now, striding purposefully through an airport or lobby, their slim wheeled suitcase whirring quietly across the polished floor, smartphone holstered like a six-gun and smart watch monitoring every breath, every step, and every beat of their hearts.

These are the sons and daughters of Thomas Watson, the man who made IBM, and, in a number of ways, invented American corporate culture. Watson and his namesake son defined what big business looked like (gray suit, white shirt, "sincere" necktie), acted like (sober, solicitous, professional) and thought like (confident, solution-oriented, goal-driven).

For three decades after the Second World War, IBM churned out super salespeople, mighty managers, and corporate captains assured in the very American belief that there was no problem that couldn't be solved with enough technology, resources, and organization.

And few of the heirs of Watson fit the mold better than Henry Ross Perot, who took the IBM way to a multibillion-dollar fortune and, but for a terribly un–Big Blue breakdown, a real shot at the presidency of these United States.

Perot was the perfect IBM recruit when he arrived. An Eagle Scout from a two-horse town in Texas who had out-hustled, outsold, and outworked his way from a junior college into Annapolis, he was eager to please and thrived in hierarchies.

Short in stature, Perot was long in confidence and an earnestly enthusiastic salesman, and the Navy gave him a berth greeting dignitaries, one of whom was an IBM man. In Perot's recollection, recounted to his many biographers, the IBM man took a shine to the young lieutenant and invited Perot to look him up when his service was up.

Perot had hit the sweet spot in his service. He graduated from the academy in 1953 after the Korean conflict had ended but mustered out in 1957 before the escalation in Vietnam. And he arrived in the business world at exactly the moment when American profit margins were as tall as the fins on a DeSoto.

"Things were so good in those days at IBM that a salesman could get rich as long as he didn't get drunk during the day," Perot said in one interview. "It didn't take a miracle worker to get somewhere."

Now, don't mistake that for humility on Perot's part. He wasn't saying that anyone could accumulate a net worth of a billion dollars (at least on paper) before their fortieth birthday. He was just saying that he wasn't too impressed with his peers at IBM, be they drunk or sober.

Even if he worked in the computer industry, Perot never presented himself as a wiz kid. Instead, he thought the wiz kids were part of the problem. There was almost always an obvious solution just at hand, but not the will to make it happen. Remember, this was a guy who promised that he would have the federal government shipshape *before* his inauguration.

"There are great plans lying all over Washington nobody ever executes," candidate Perot said. "It's like having a blueprint for a house you never built. You don't have anywhere to sleep."

He would be the builder because he was willing to do the work.

Todd Mason, who covered Perot for *Businessweek*, wrote an unauthorized biography of the surprising southern tech billionaire in 1990, just as public fascination with the cantankerous Texan was starting to reach feverish levels.

Mason describes the way his subject made his mark when he signed on in IBM's Dallas office:

Sales trainee Perot showed his mettle from the start. During his training, Perot stepped into the breach at a difficult installation at a trucking firm. At one critical point, he moved a cot into the computer room. He was feeding data into the machine, a task that took days. When the card reader stopped clicking, Perot would wake up and feed it another stack. "Right away you think this guy is not run-of-the- mill," says Dean Campbell, a retired IBM salesman.

Indeed he was not. Perot, by his own telling, would hit his sales target—IBM's 100 Percent Club—in his first year and every year thereafter. And every year, he was hitting his quotas sooner. But in 1960, the company changed its policy and put a cap on commissions beyond a salesperson's quota. Perot told people he maxed out for 1961 on the nineteenth of January.

Now, please bear with me for this next bit of corporate lore. For those of you who are not businessmen or businesswomen, these are the kinds of stories that make up the secular faith of American industry. And in Perot's case, it may actually be true.

By his telling, Perot had grown frustrated with his maxed-out commissions and his lunkheaded boss's refusal to embrace his big idea for IBM. He wanted the company to sell customers bigger computers than they needed and then lease out time on the machines to companies that couldn't afford large capital investments.

Remember, this was when businesses ran on adding machines, carbon paper, and telephone switchboards. Access to a computer by lease would have been a godsend to many smaller firms. IBM would profit at every turn: the sale, the service, the software, and administering the system rentals. It was a genius idea, if he did say so himself.

Perot's boss was by no means impressed. The company was hugely profitable, hyper-dominant in its sector, and did not need to get into the business of leasing out Hollerith punch card readers for small profits. He told his thirty-one-year-old salesman to stay in his own lane.

A frustrated Perot, whose haircut has never much departed from the USNA requirement buzz cut, went to see the barber.

There is an old saying: When the student is ready, the teacher will appear. And for Perot the teacher would be a quote from Henry David Thoreau in a *Reader's Digest* in a Dallas barbershop. The magazine, which sits in a glass-encased place of honor in the headquarters of the company he founded, told him this: "The mass of men lead lives of quiet desperation."

Bang! There and then, Perot decided that he would not be one of those quietly desperate fools, toiling away in what the world called resignation, but Thoreau said was really "confirmed desperation."

It is good for Perot that he found Thoreau in digest form. If he'd have met the author in the original, the young capitalist might have gotten to the part about "None can be an impartial or wise observer of human life but from the vantage ground of what we should call voluntary poverty."

(Perot also definitely never got around to "Civil Disobedience," either: "A government in which the majority rule in all cases cannot be based on justice, even as far as men understand it.")

No, Perot was not interested in poverty, voluntary or otherwise. And with $1,000 he said was borrowed from his wife's wages as a schoolteacher, he set out into the corporate wilderness.

Perot had married his wife, Margot, six years prior in her coal-country hometown of Greenburg, Pennsylvania. When Perot ran for president, the *Washington Post* would call her "oblivious" and "Blondie to his Dagwood" in what was supposed to be a flattering profile. Articles sneered broadly at the fact that she considered her five children a modest brood.

(Our knowledge of Mrs. Perot is limited because, among the great number of subjects on which she and her husband seemed to agree, one was that it was important for her to not be part of the public rationale for his candidacy. He said he didn't even consult with her on his decision to run.)

But with her money, trust, and unwavering support the young salesman started his firm, Electronic Data Services, on his thirty-second birthday, June 27, 1962.

Here's the part where corporate creation myths collide with American political history. How did Ross Perot make his billions? Was he an upstart who blew up the business world as we know it, or was he one of the most successful remoras that fed on an increasingly fat and prosperous federal government shark?

As you can guess by now, the answer is a little of both.

We don't have any reason to disbelieve Perot's account of EDS's founding, and none of his biographers disagree.

Perot worked for five months paying only a secretary ($1,000 stretched a good deal longer on labor costs fifty-six years ago) and getting absolutely stone cold shut out. He told one biographer that it was seventy-eight times, but regardless of the number, the message from companies was the same: It was not happening. Not owning the equipment and convincing smaller companies to buy time on bigger companies' machines did not work.

What might've been an interesting idea with IBM was not very useful if all you were was a guy with a close-cropped haircut and an idea about how a client should spend $1.6 million so that he could sell time on a machine he could not afford.

Now, this is the part in the corporate success story in which the individual faces resistance to his or her idea and proceeds anyway, in spite of the evidence to the contrary believed by unthinking people, and ends up being proven right by the same hierarchy he disdained.

Perot may not have been an IBM man anymore, but he carried the mark of one. And there were millions of them and their coreligionists from other companies that had learned the IBM way by then. Some were lesser and some were greater. Some were like Robert McNamara and Lee Iacocca. Some were like Preston Tucker and John DeLorean.

We call them members of the "silent generation" now, but if they were quiet, it was only because they were too busy trying to make money talk. And lordy day, could Perot make money.

After all those months scrounging and getting rejected, Perot landed a contract with Frito-Lay. He got the deal less than two years before Frito-Lay was bought out by Pepsi, making it part of one of the largest food conglomerates in the United States. Silicon Valley may have been thinking about microchips by then, but Perot was thinking about potato chips. His company (now bought and sold and renamed many times) still calls Frito-Lay's hometown, the Dallas suburb of Plano, home.

If Perot had gone on from there to reinvent technology and revolutionize American industry (or even just potato chips) with new computers and new systems, this would be an unambiguous story as it relates to Perot the future politician. But Perot was not an innovator; he was an excavator. The way he found his riches was by digging deep into the federal government.

About the same time that Perot was getting started, Lyndon Johnson's Great Society was getting going, too. Depending on your point of view, Medicare and Medicaid may or may not be good ways to deliver health care to old people and poor people. But they were most definitely a boon to people who sold large, already technologically stagnant computer systems.

Federal health insurance is technically administered by the states (a concession made to southern and moderate Democrats and the one Republican who voted for the legislation). But in order to get the federal money to come in, the states have to follow strict rules and provide all kinds of information about who got what, what went where, and how much it cost.

This created an astonishing market for people selling computers, and Perot got after it in a big way.

Perot hustled his idea for selling computing services rather than computers, which we would come to know as outsourcing, into a $350 million fortune (again, on paper) before the 1960s were over. He did it by taking his company public at a time when most medium-sized companies like his did not. But he also did it by never-say-die salesmanship and sheer intensity.

CEO Perot hired very deliberately, almost to the point of peculiarity. There was a certain type of man he wanted for his company, a variant of the IBM ideal. But he upgraded the basic model with his own workaholic drive and fanatical competitiveness. "I am looking for people who love to win," he liked to say. "If I run out of those, I want people who hate to lose."

His salesmen went out, plowed into the fertile fields of the welfare state, and grew their boss a fortune. Perot was free to start tweaking the corporate culture of his creation. He wanted a dress code stricter than the one at IBM—facial hair was forbidden and hairstyles had to fall within corporate specifications—and an incentive system that rewarded cutthroats.

He was also becoming accustomed to getting his way.

On a rare visit back to Texarkana, Perot saw that the house where he grew up had been painted white. He found the literal whitewashing of his youth unacceptable, so he bought the house and ordered a crew to scrape the paint from the bricks. Informed that it was impossible, he had another idea. He would later recall his answer to an interviewer: "Then take out all the bricks and turn them around."

Most Americans, though, didn't have any reason to know about this idiosyncratic Texas tycoon. That would change in the holiday season of 1969 when Perot took a gamble with global geopolitical consequences: He was going to try to bring Christmas to the fourteen hundred or so American POWs in North Vietnam.

While Perot was busy building better mousetraps, a lot of his classmates from the Naval Academy were fighting the

Vietnam War. Because a large number of the men the North Vietnamese took captive were pilots shot down on bombing raids launched from aircraft carriers, many of them were naval officers.

Perot had become increasingly focused on the plight of these men. By then, the cruelty and inhumane treatment of the American prisoners was well known, and their release was becoming a pivotal part of the Nixon administration's efforts to negotiate an end to the war. Frustrated by the status quo, Perot put his mind and money to work.

He formed a nonprofit group, United We Stand, and began looking for ways to apply public pressure on the government in Hanoi and its benefactors in Beijing and Moscow. A letter-writing campaign came first, but then came a more audacious plan to airlift Christmas presents to those imprisoned.

Perot leased two jets, which he dubbed "Peace on Earth" and "Goodwill Toward Men," to carry more than twenty-five tons of gifts, medicine, and meals to the POWs. Perot flew aboard the first one to Bangkok, where he began negotiating with the North Vietnamese for the privilege of entering their airspace.

On the other side of the world, Perot deployed a group of prisoners' wives to the Paris peace talks between Secretary of State Henry Kissinger and his North Vietnamese counterpart to plead their case. Perot was treating this like one of his sales pitches: Work every angle and never give up.

He was racing the clock since the North Vietnamese were going to stop accepting Christmas gifts for the prisoners on

December 31. So on Christmas Day, Perot directed his plane to Laos for more negotiations, and then back to Bangkok when those failed. He started talking to the Soviets about their delivering the packages. He then ordered the jet to Copenhagen so he would be ready to head to Moscow on a moment's notice.

The mission failed. But it was such an audacious failure that it became an international news story, especially because reporters loved the twangy Texan and his colorful quotes. Perot may not have gotten the Christmas presents in, but he certainly helped increase the pressure on North Vietnam over its mistreatment of prisoners.

Perot would stay on it, organizing more relief missions and publicity campaigns, and even offering to pay a $100 million ransom. By the time North Vietnam was ready to release the prisoners in 1973, Perot had become synonymous with the cause.

Five years later, when two of Perot's employees were taken prisoner by the revolutionary government in Iran, he was ready not just to apply what he learned tangling with the North Vietnamese, but to raise the stakes. He hired and extensively equipped a team of commandos to set the men free. After training at Perot's weekend retreat outside Dallas, the team headed for Tehran.

Perot meanwhile went to Tehran on his own to visit his employees and continue negotiations with their captors. When those failed, the hired guns went to work. Rather than shooting their way in, though, they helped stir up an angry mob demanding the release of Iranian political prisoners. In the chaos, the two EDS employees were able to escape. The commandos were able to spirit them out of the country and across the border into Turkey.

The story was a media sensation. Perot got wall-to-wall coverage for the feat. Author Ken Follett turned the story into a bestselling book, which NBC made into a smash television miniseries in the spring of 1986. And by then, Perot had a fortune to match his fame.

Perot wasn't *really* rich until General Motors bought him out. In those days, GM knew it was dying. Like a slightly more intellectual brontosaurus, it was enjoying the fruits of success, but aware of the impending asteroid collision. Its response was to try to diversify, with a particular focus on technology. Having been told that Perot's outsourcing company was innovative, but not too innovative, GM wanted in.

GM paid $2.4 billion in 1984 for a controlling share of EDS. Perot also snagged enough GM stock to instantly become the company's single largest shareholder. Now fifty-four, he had joined the ranks of the super-rich.

Through his work as a government contractor and then through his POW efforts, Perot had cultivated lots of connections in the world of politics and government. He was already a heavy hitter in Texas politics by dint of his wealth and influence, but he was ready to start shaping national politics in a more deliberate way.

Fortunately for him, there was a very efficient way to do that, thanks to the accelerating adoption of cable television.

In 1980, there were sixteen million cable subscribers, mostly in dense regional clusters. By 1990, cable was in fifty-three million households, beaming some eighty networks into homes across the country. A channel for sports, a channel for pop music, a channel for history, and on and on and on...

For people who came of age after the mid-1990s, it may be hard to imagine, but this was nothing less than a revolution in the way Americans consumed information. After five decades of near-total control, the big three broadcast networks were losing their hold.

Nowhere was the change more striking than with news. Ted Turner, a man not unlike Perot—a quirky, ambitious southerner with revolutionary ambitions—was making it happen. Turner's idea of a twenty-four-hour news channel had initially sounded laughable. Television stations typically provided only a couple of hours of news programming a day. Who would sit and watch the news around the clock?

The first Iraq war answered that question in 1990. Americans had seen lots of television coverage of Vietnam, but this war would be broadcast live every minute of every day. It was a ratings bonanza for CNN and launched many of its anchors and correspondents into instant celebrity.

Larry King had been doing a televised version of his successful radio talk show on CNN since the mid-1980s, but with its increased viewership and influence, CNN now provided King with a remarkable platform to shape the national discussion. And Perot was one of his favorite guests.

Perot had long been a fixture of broadcast news morning

chat shows and even Phil Donahue's syndicated daytime show, but *Larry King Live* was the perfect place for him. He was able to hold forth on the news of the day, but increasingly turned his focus toward what he said was the unconscionable stupidity of the federal government and its leaders.

He had lots of opinions, all of which he shared without hesitation. He wanted term limits and a balanced federal budget. And he had particular disdain for two of the initiatives most dear to then-president George H. W. Bush: a free-trade pact with Mexico and Canada and the war with Iraq.

By this point, Perot was thinking seriously about a presidential run. His United We Stand group, founded to increase public pressure for the return of the POWs, was already turning toward a new kind of grassroots organizing mission: to create a groundswell for Perot's political ambitions.

That's not to say that Perot's grassroots were all Astroturf. As he laid out his political vision in television interviews, and sometimes in thirty-minute-long infomercials he paid for himself, he was generating huge ratings.

King bragged to the *New York Times* about the phenomenon, saying that "television will elect the next President."

And cable television was part of Perot's policy pitch, too. His most ambitious proposal was to use the power of television to govern the country. Along with protectionist trade policies and government efficiency reforms, he also proposed that the government should use televised town halls to introduce direct democracy on the federal level for the first time.

The idea was pretty straightforward. The president,

whomever he might be (wink, wink), would periodically take to the airwaves and offer sets of proposals for addressing various concerns. After describing the options, the president would invite voters to electronically submit their opinions. Press 1 to join NAFTA, press 2 to stay out.

These electronic town halls became as much a part of Perot's platform as deficits and trade. He argued, as did many at the time, that lobbyists and special interest groups were crowding out the voices of the electorate. He believed that armed with vox populi, presidents could smash through legislative gridlock and start setting things right. And if that meant changing the Constitution to apply the force of law to these televised plebiscites, so be it.

The momentum, real and manufactured, for Perot's candidacy continued to grow until February 20, 1992, when he appeared on King's show to announce not a campaign but a challenge: If his supporters could collect enough signatures and do enough legwork to get his name on the ballot in all fifty states, then Perot would run.

The ballot drive became a consuming story in the political press. There was drama and suspense about the signature drive and, of course, the fascinating yes-no-maybe so candidate in the middle of it.

His incipient campaign, though, drew a different kind of scrutiny than Perot was accustomed to. And what had been endearing—or at least nonthreatening—in an opinionated billionaire television guest was less charming in a man with a chance to be president.

Political biographer David Remnick found on a visit to Perot's headquarters that there were darker things on the mind of the man of the hour:

> One afternoon in his office, he started describing to me what he said was a "conspiracy inside the Pentagon" to cover up alleged sightings of American prisoners in Vietnam. Perot would brook no disagreement on the subject and, at one point, went into his office safe to retrieve a snapshot of a defense official and a young Asian woman—a photograph, Perot insisted darkly, that "completely compromised" the Pentagon. "Okay, now you see what I mean?" Perot said. I have not seen a smile of such self-assurance since; or not until recently, and it belonged to Oliver Stone.

These warning signs didn't do any harm to the support for Perot's candidacy that spring, though.

In May, the public fascination with Perot was still growing—and so were his poll numbers. Gallup found Bush and Perot tied at 35 percent, with Democratic nominee Bill Clinton 10 points behind then. But by the end of the first week of June, Perot was still picking up steam and had moved out to a 4-point lead over Bush, still at 35 percent, and Clinton, still languishing at 25 percent.

In anticipation of his success at getting on the ballot, Perot hired a campaign team. Whether it was busting employees out of an Iranian prison or winning the presidency, Perot wanted the best hired guns he could get. He picked a top Republican, Ed Rollins, who had run Ronald Reagan's 1984 landslide-winning campaign; and a top Democrat, Hamilton Jordan, who had engineered Jimmy Carter's underdog victory in the 1980 primaries. Perot said he would hire the best people from both parties to run the government, and he wanted his campaign to be a down payment on the idea.

But he made it clear to them that he would not fulfill the normal duties of a candidate, even if he was building out a more typical campaign apparatus. There would be no scripted messaging, no retail politicking, and none of the warm and fuzzy image makeovers that consultants believed he needed. Clinton could go on Arsenio Hall and play the saxophone if he wanted to, but with Perot it was going to be all about the flip charts. Any question about his personal life or his feelings or his family was met with a scoff.

"This campaign is about issues," Perot would say again and again. "That's a distraction."

It was an unwieldy arrangement, to say the least: two campaign managers, a candidate who refused to be managed, and a grassroots operation being run out of a separate enterprise over which the candidate had total control and with which the campaign could not coordinate. And United We Stand was calling the shots.

Rollins and Jordan, though, couldn't complain about their place in the race or the chance to make political history. The two-party system, which had been trudging along since the days of Andy Jackson, looked ready to tip over.

A Pew Research survey on the race showed where Perot's burgeoning support was coming from. The businessman was doing gangbusters with better-educated, more affluent voters in the Midwest and West. And while Perot fared better with men (39 percent), he was still outperforming Clinton and Bush among female voters (33 percent).

And most remarkable, when Pew tested the race with different sets of voters, they found that Perot was drawing equally from Republicans and Democrats. The sons and daughters of Thomas Watson recognized the arrival of one of their own.

Perot was brusque bordering on authoritarian in his approach, and it seemed to connect with voters. Pew asked respondents, "Some people feel that what this country needs is some really strong leadership that would try to solve problems directly without worrying how Congress and the Supreme Court might feel. Others think that such strong leadership might be dangerous. Which one is closer to what you think?"

Sixty-three percent of voters in the late spring of 1992 said it was time for a bulldozer presidency. And Perot was ready to oblige.

Perot had given scant attention or thought to many issues outside of his own fascinations. But social and cultural issues are the beating heart of politics in a way that trade, spending, and taxes never will be. Perot did not let his inexperience with these issues prevent him from having opinions.

- *On abortion:* "I support federal funding of abortions for poor women. Since these women have already made the decision, for public health reasons, we should ensure that the procedure is done safely."

- *On gay and lesbian Americans serving in his administration:* "I don't want anybody there that will be a point of controversy with the American people. It will distract from the work to be done."
- *On the war on drugs:* "You can declare civil war and the drug dealer is the enemy. There ain't no bail... [drug dealers] go to POW camp. You can start dealing with the problem in straight military terms."

Perot would drop these bombs without discussing the matter with his campaign, but then hide behind it when the entirely predictable backlash followed.

But mostly Perot stuck to his core issue set: using the power of the government to reinvent the American economy. As he said, "Force on new industries of the future to make sure we nail those for our country."

The Constitution, however, presented some problems here, too. "Germany and Japan are winning," Perot said. "Why are they winning? They got new constitutions in 1945. Our Constitution was written two hundred years ago, before [the Industrial Revolution] occurred."

Germany and Japan may not really have been winning. But it was a commonly held belief at the time that America was about to be supplanted by one of the growing economic superpowers. America had won the Cold War, but would see one of our competitors reap the benefits. It sounds silly now given what has transpired in those two countries, but smart people actually believed these things back then.

Perot wanted a system in which the federal government and big business worked together to arrange the American economy. He wanted to grant broad new powers to the government for making these arrangements, but also to bring the best in big business into the government to set policies. The ideal situation, he said, would produce maximum employment and minimum inequality and would guarantee American economic dominance for generations more.

What Watson had done for IBM and American industry, Perot was going to make the official policy of government. He was tired of all of the mistakes and experiments. It was time for *correct* answers, forcefully imposed.

In a 2018 interview with *The Economist*, hedge fund hotshot turned Washington hot mess Anthony Scaramucci said of his erstwhile boss Donald Trump that Trump's presidency could be considered a success if in a decade or so the emperor of Amazon, Jeff Bezos, was president.

Some politicians and pundits today speak longingly of the business/government symbiosis of China. They sound like how Perot spoke of Japan's cartel-based economy twenty-five years ago.

We can't compete, they say, because our system is too outmoded, too focused on individuality, and too much geared toward conflict to innovate the way China, or whatever the perceived threat of the moment may be, does.

Americans instinctively recoil from the idea of cartels

and oligarchy, so the solution for the pro-business populist is pretty straightforward: Convince the people to demand it. If you believe that what really ails the country is insufficient wealth, and you have the personal resources to shape public opinion, as Perot did, you might just try to start a revolution.

You would explain the problems to the ordinary people in ways that they could understand, and then use their mandate to rule in benevolent but authoritarian fashion. And you wouldn't really be a dictator because you would always be subject to the call of the voters.

As our old pal Huey Long said, "A man is not a dictator when he is given a commission from the people and carries it out."

Here's where it gets tricky, and where we run back into our original conundrum. The debate between the Founders was about how to balance the will of the people with the rule of law. Too much order, and the people are stifled by the elites. Too much popular control, and the people are crushed by the tyranny of the mob.

But what happens when the elites become good at manipulating the mob? We think of American demagoguery with men like Long, ranting and raving, or of Trump and Barack Obama standing before tens of thousands of worshipful followers making fantastic promises and pleas to emotionality.

What about a "guy with a bad accent and boring flip charts," as Perot called himself? In this century, the next steps toward the end of republicanism might not be giving spittle-splattering speeches denouncing the courts and

Congress. They may come in simple suits with quiet board-room voices, sliding imperceptibly into your immersive media consumption.

Michael Bloomberg wants to give voice to the popular out-cry for gun control measures. And if there isn't one, he'll produce it. Mark Zuckerberg wants to help empower democracy, but first needs to set a few ground rules about what is and isn't a "positive" idea for consideration. Larry Page and Sergey Brin want to use Google's technology to make government more responsive to citizens, but still maintain control over the spigot that directs popular opinion.

It's an idea as old as self-government. Aristotle envisioned a world that Perot and today's tech titans would like: "We all agree that the most excellent man should rule." But how shall we measure excellence? And what shall we do when the men reveal themselves to be tyrants, not benevolent rulers? And what do we do when they use their bully pulpit to perpetuate their power?

Aggressive pragmatism is always appealing, just so long as you are the one deciding what's pragmatic and how aggressively to pursue it.

But in the seven or eight weeks that he was a declared, competitive candidate for the presidency, Perot had managed to convince as much as 40 percent of the electorate that he was the correct instrument for scraping the whitewash off of Washington.

As it turned out, though, it was more than Perot could handle.

First, his staff imploded. Rollins was forced out on July 15 after losing a showdown with the ballot access team. (Rollins later revealed that one of the Perotists had accused him of being a CIA plant sent by Bush to sabotage the campaign.) Jordan was now the last campaign manager standing, but he knew that he would likely face the same fate soon enough. For a guy who was campaigning on putting the experts in charge, Perot was not interested in listening to them when it came to his campaign.

Jordan didn't have to worry for long, though. The very next day, July 16, Perot dropped out of the race that he had never officially joined.

You can just guess where Perot went to make this announcement. When King asked him why he was getting out, Perot offered some argle-bargle about the Electoral College and not wanting to throw the race to the House of Representatives. And that was it. Millions of dollars and millions of signatures later, Perot said he was walking away.

All at once, the race was reset. While it had been unclear before which side Perot was hurting the most, it became clear at once that Clinton—a moderate-sounding, pragmatic southern Democrat—had been the disadvantaged party. His numbers shot through the roof when Perot left the race. According to Gallup, Clinton went from about a quarter of the vote in a three-man race in June to 57 percent in a head-to-head race with Bush in July.

While Perot was out, his organization wasn't. In September, United We Stand announced that Perot was on the ballot in all fifty states. Perot wouldn't commit to running, but he was willing to start playing footsie with supporters again, hinting that he might respond to the call of the people. It takes real chutzpah to convince people to draft you for president *twice*.

On October 1, Perot did get back in the race, this time officially. But much of his support had evaporated. His sudden departure had reinforced the major parties' narrative that he was too odd a duck to be president. Luckily for Perot, though, he arrived with enough support and in enough time to participate in the three presidential debates.

The debates did deal Perot a bad blow when his hastily selected running mate, retired admiral James Stockdale, cratered in his contest with Vice President Dan Quayle and Senator Al Gore. Perot had named Stockdale, one of the POWs he had worked to free from North Vietnam, as a placeholder back in March in order to meet ballot access rules.

When Perot jumped back in the race, it was too late to try to switch, which left the career military man to melt under the hot lights of the debate. His opening lines—"Who am I? Why am I here?"—intended as a jocular way to address his status as an unknown in the race, are still remembered as one of the worst utterances in political history.

But Perot slayed.

Compared to the painfully stiff Bush and the overwhelming odor of baloney coming off of Clinton, Perot sounded reasonable and authentic. His numbers didn't reach their prior strength, but he rebounded and pushed Clinton into a competitive race with Bush again.

Perot was not done dropping bombs, though. Eight days before the election, he appeared on *60 Minutes* to reveal the *real* story of his departure from the race. And it was a doozy. The Bush campaign, he said, had used the CIA to make computer alterations to a photograph of his daughter in order to disrupt her wedding in August of that year.

Another of Perot's daughters told reporters the next day on the campaign trail that she believed the photo was doctored to make her sister appear to have been a lesbian, but the candidate refused to say just what the dirty trick was, just that the Bush/CIA folks had the means to "put a head on another body" in a photograph.

Perot also accused Bush of wiretapping his office and said that "a source" had given him "a floor plan, layout of my floor, and telephone numbers [the Bush/CIA operatives] wanted to tap."

And that was plenty to kill off any new momentum for Perot. He did manage to win 19 percent of the popular vote the next week, but didn't get close to a single electoral vote anywhere. Clinton beat Bush by 6 points in the popular vote and carried thirty-two states. It wasn't even close.

Perot would run again four years later with even less success and would also found the Reform Party out of his United We Stand enterprise. The party didn't add up to much, but did retain federal matching funds and ballot access from the 1992 effort.

Perot's party did help get a former professional wrestler elected as governor of Minnesota, but by its 2000 presidential primary, the Reform Party was such a carnival that it quickly vanished from public view. The shift to national security concerns following 9/11 left little appetite for amateurism in the electorate.

But one of the 2000 Reform Party contenders, also a billionaire and an inveterate talk show trouper and conspiracy theorist, would reappear on the political stage more than a decade later as a Republican and win the White House.

Perot's movement didn't make it, but the idea that America is so badly off that it needs a tough businessman to smash through the system, even if it's messy or stretches beyond the limits of the Constitution, would come to be a defining force in our politics.

Trump may not match Watson's idea of an IBM man, but like Perot, he certainly understands the allure of the idea that the correct answers aren't that hard to come by. You've just got to sell them.

Conclusion

I hope we all keep some moments from American history close to our hearts—stories from our shared past that affirm our values and keep us hopeful in times of difficulty.

For me there are many. But there is one that calls me back over and over, urging me to pick it up and reconsider its beauty and what it says about the country I love.

The election of 1864 remains to me a moment of triumph with which very few can compare. Can you imagine leaders in another nation shattered by an ongoing civil war, voluntarily staging free, fair, and full elections? I find it perpetually amazing that we did so without governmental interference and that the losers accepted the verdict of the voters.

If ever the country was ripe for a demagogue, it was at that moment. And Abraham Lincoln possessed many of the qualities a demagogue might need. He was from humble beginnings, he possessed extraordinary abilities to understand and manipulate the sentiments of others, and he had a gift for language few leaders of any generation could claim.

After his unlikely rise to power, the start of the war would have given him all he needed to assume nearly dictatorial powers. Certainly Republicans in Congress would have backed him in anything that was aimed at crushing the rebellion as swiftly and brutally as possible.

Yet Lincoln risked his own reelection and thereby the war

effort itself by fighting against those in Congress and across his party who wanted to preserve the Union at the expense of the Constitution.

In the first year of the war, Washington was at risk from saboteurs in Maryland. So Lincoln invoked the constitutional clause allowing him to suspend the right to legal due process "in Cases of Rebellion or Invasion [when] the public Safety may require." The army was thereby allowed to arrest and indefinitely detain Confederates and sympathizers, those whom we might call "enemy combatants" today.

To Lincoln's dismay, martial law became only too popular with Republicans in border states, especially Missouri. The power to jail dissidents, it turns out, tends to sit very comfortably in leaders' hands. As one St. Louis newspaper correspondent put it:

> So far from being unpopular, it is believed that a large portion of our loyal people are willing to see a provision incorporated in the charter of the city, requiring six months of martial law to be imposed...every five years to clean up all the little cases of outraged justice, loose indictments, public corruption, and private peculation, which the ordinary courts cannot reach.

By the closing months of the war, Lincoln had to send the regular army to Missouri to force the local government and militia to reinstate due process.

Lincoln may ultimately have sided with the radical Republicans on the need to obliterate the rebellion and in their aim of abolishing slavery. But like the conservatives in Congress, he knew that those aims could not come at the price of unraveling the Constitution.

Our charter had been in place only seventy-three years when the Civil War began—a timespan comparable to our own distance now from the end of World War II. The primacy and inviolability of the Constitution were not the established concepts that they are today.

Just before his first inauguration, Lincoln received a delegation from a peace conference being held at the Willard Hotel in Washington. The conferees had struck upon a constitutionally dubious compromise that they believed might avert the war. By meeting some demands of the slave states, secession might be avoided.

Lincoln played it cool with the delegates, calmly hearing their case. Among their number was one of New York's richest men, William Dodge, who demanded that Lincoln assent to what amounted to extortion by the South lest war consume the country and disrupt trade. He feared, he said, that "grass will grow in the streets of our commercial cities."

Lincoln, who did not once raise his voice, made himself completely clear:

> I will, to the best of my ability, preserve, protect, and defend the Constitution of the United States.... It is not the Constitution as I would like to have it, but as it is, that is to be defended. The Constitution will not be preserved and defended until it is enforced and obeyed in every part of every one of the United States. It must

be so respected, obeyed, enforced, and defended, and let the grass grow where it may.

An observer recalled that Lincoln's impromptu remarks "fell and fitted as the light does," and that everyone present knew in that moment that he would not be moved. Lincoln had decided that America would remain a federal republic, or die trying.

And when, four awful years later, Lincoln submitted himself and his aims to a war-weary nation, it was widely assumed that voters would reject his narrow view about preserving the republic at all costs. Democrats were running a candidate who pledged compromise, peaceful reunion, and an end to the horrific bloodshed.

But voters affirmed Lincoln's trust in them and the Constitution, giving him the mandate he needed to bring the war to a close. Lincoln had not told them what they wanted to hear nor promised comfort when hardship was inevitable, and yet they stuck with him anyway.

At the outset of this book, I observed that populist revolts are most likely to arise when the balance between the competing ideas of our founding—freedom and order—is broken.

Never has it been so badly broken as it was in Lincoln's day. But even in this far less troubled time of ours, his remedy remains available. Our Constitution can still help us restore that balance, but only if it is "respected, obeyed, enforced, and defended."

Doing so not only provides a safeguard against demagogues like a few of the folks we met in these pages but reduces the want of them in the people.

Acknowledgments

The first acknowledgment is simple, since if it weren't for Dana Perino, this book never would have come to pass. She is the absolute instigator, so blame her if you didn't like it!

Dana has been a stalwart champion of my work, a great sounding board, a commiserating fellow author, and an occasional kick in the hindquarters. She is also one of the most marvelous friends I have ever been blessed to have. She really has become another sister to me.

One of her many gifts to me has been getting to know the generous, patient editor for this book, Sean Desmond. The tender ministrations of Sean and the team at Twelve made this book come to life. It's a privilege to work with people who care about the value of words and ideas.

In my career, I have been blessed to have had several great bosses and mentors, and I definitely hit pay dirt with Bill Sammon. As my managing editor at Fox News, Bill exemplifies the kind of newsman that everyone in this business should aspire to be. As my friend and confidant, Bill has given me the benefit of his many trips up the bestseller lists in working out this book. He's been an absolute North Star for me.

It's hard for me to believe that I am fortunate to work with so many wonderful people all at once here in the Fox News Washington Bureau. People like Brit Hume, Bryan Boughton, Cherie Grzech, Bret Baier, Doug Rohrbeck, Jake Gibson, and many others past and present have taught me so much about American politics. I'm honored beyond words to work here and call people like these my colleagues.

Fox News has given me the chance to do what I absolutely consider to be the greatest job in the world. Thank goodness Rupert Murdoch didn't know how to take no for an answer when the world said it couldn't be done.

Special thanks to my colleague Brianna McClelland, who endured me in varying states of incapacity, distraction, and exhaustion as I was finishing the book—days when our daily *Halftime Report* newsletter slipped into overtime.

I owe a huge debt to Charlie Hurt, Washington's leading Anti-Federalist, with whom I have for years been able to hash out these conflicts. Charlie was especially helpful in my writing about Huey Long and George Wallace. My dear friend's fundamental decency as a man kept me from lapsing into hyperbole when exploring the defects of Southern populists. I often kept my adjectives in check by wondering how they would sound in his ears.

Thanks also to my friend Jonah Goldberg, who was eager to aid me in my work and readily provided a banquet of resources about American populism from his own research on the subject. Some crumbs from that feast you see assembled in these pages. He's a good and generous man.

And certainly none of this would have been possible without Stephen G. Smith, who was my editor at the *Washington Examiner*. I needed a job and he needed a political editor, but Stephen was still taking a big chance on a kid from West Virginia without any national experience. Steve's gifts as an editor surpass any I have known, and his belief that somehow I could be even a little part of the national conversation was a turning point in my career.

But there are a couple of voices I hear every time I put fingers to keyboard. One is Bob Kelly, who taught me a master class in political journalism. Every time the sentences are getting tangled up and the lede is sinking under an avalanche of adjectives, I can hear Bob telling me "C'mon, Boudreaux, how about keep it simple?" I still don't know why he called me Boudreaux, but Bob is sorely missed.

The other is my dad. He knew the difference between the country and its government, and he raised me to maintain a healthy skepticism about anyone who sought to wield power. He also knew that the best defense against the pretentions of those who would make themselves our masters was to laugh at them. When I see some puffed-up freshman congressman making pious pronouncements or a presidential candidate making ridiculous promises, I think how Beez would have roared with laughter at the foolishness of it all.

And maybe that's what we need a good dose of these days. Politics is too important to take so seriously.

Index

About the Author

Chris Stirewalt joined Fox News Channel in July of 2010 and serves as politics editor based in Washington, D.C. Stirewalt authors the daily *Fox News Halftime Report* political news note, and he co-hosts the hit podcast *Perino & Stirewalt: I'll Tell You What.*